Arabic Made easy:

100 Verbs in Context

A Beginner's guide to the Arabic language

and all of its keys

Malik Selim

SPECIAL BONUS!

Want this book for FREE?

Get FREE, unlimited access to it and all of my new books by joining the Fan Base!

Table of contents

<u>Introduction</u>

Arabic is a language that is, in my opinion, one of the world's most distinct and powerful languages today. If you didn't know, Arabic is now one of the top ten most widely spoken languages globally, with over 230 million native speakers spread around the globe. There are also additional 100-200 million people who speak it as a second language throughout northern Africa and western Asia. It's worth noting that the Arabic language has a variety of dialects. However, we will focus on Modern Standard Arabic (MSA) in this book, which has a unique status as the formal written standard for the media, culture, and education in the Arab world.

You might be wondering why, with so many various dialects and varieties of the Arabic language, you're focused on the modern standard Arabic (MSA) out of all of them. It is critical to understand that the Arab world's official language is Modern Standard Arabic. Furthermore, though there are some changes in terminology among the various dialects, all of the terms in the other cultures are derived in some way from modern standard Arabic (MSA). It is the starting point for all dialects. As a result, studying modern standard Arabic first is far more effective and relevant for a complete beginner. Suppose you are interested in learning various Arabic dialects. In such a case, this book is an excellent place to start, as it includes a list of the 100 most important basic verbs for any Arabic speaker.

In the past, I've seen a lot of Arabic learning books. Some are good, while others are bad. However, one recurring theme I've noticed throughout these books and guidelines is that most of them overlook the significance of CONTEXT. Because the Arabic language is known for having one of the world's largest, if not the largest, vocabularies. The most widely used Arabic dictionary among Arabs today, generally known as العرب لسان, has over 100,000 real USABLE words!

That being said, learning that many words in any language is not a realistic expectation for anyone. This is where the importance of context becomes apparent. There are around 9200 viable consonant roots in the Arabic language (In العرب لسان). Arabic words are made up of three- and four-letter consonant roots that define the word's underlying meaning. With the addition of vowels, prefixes, and suffixes, each collection of root letters can provide a large number of words with similar meanings. They are all, however, related to the three- or four-letter root verb. For e.g

The root verb – بَ—تَ—ك which means to write, prescribe, to dictate (depending on the context)

some of the derivatives of this three-letter root verb are:

كِتَابٌ – A book

كِتَابَة – The act of writing

كَاتِبٌ – A male writer

كَاتِبَة – A female writer

مَكْتَبٌ – A desk

مَكْتَبَة – A bookshop/library

مَكْتُوبٌ – The thing that is written

كَتِيبَة – A brigade/Battalion

These are only a few examples; there are a lot more. So, if you can memorise and remember as many of those three and four-letter roots verbs as possible (in context), you will have the keys to thousands of Arabic words. Not only that, but in as little as 12 months, you'll be able to understand the vast majority (95%) of any Arabic conversation!

Did you realise that the Arabic word "Camel" has nearly 100 different meanings? That's correct, nearly a hundred! In the Arabic language, a verb can have several different meanings depending on the situation in which it is employed. This book will go through the 100 verbs that every new Arabic learner should know if they wish to advance in the language. Not only that, but this book will conjugate all of the verbs for you, as well as provide you with all of the verbs' definitions, contexts, and three examples of how to express the verb in a meaningful sentence.

<u>Chapter 1 – Why should I even learn Arabic?</u>

If you've already purchased this book, I'm guessing you're interested in studying Arabic. If you're still on the fence about whether or not you want to continue this path or if it's worthwhile for you, let me explain why you should study Arabic.

<u>The demand for Arabic speakers is increasing… EVERY year</u>

Arabic is an essential language for bridging the gap between the eastern and western worlds. In the western world, there is a strong demand for Arabic speakers, but only a little supply. Some countries may even provide funding to help you learn the language. Did you know that six Arabic-speaking countries are in the top 50 commodities export markets for the United Kingdom? According to the British Council, Arabic is the "second most important language of the future."

<u>The Arabic alphabet</u>

Farsi, Dari, Pashto, Urdu, Somali, Turkmen, Kazakh, Kurdish, and other languages utilise alphabets derived from the Arabic alphabet. You will be able to read these languages if you can read the Arabic script. Of course, every language has a few additional letters, and you will most likely not comprehend what you are reading, but you will be able to read it, which is a great start!

<u>Arabic has one of the richest histories.</u>

During the Middle Ages, Arabic was a significant driving force of culture in Europe and other parts. Especially in subjects like mathematics, science, and philosophy. As a result, many languages in Europe have classical Arabic words embedded into their Vocabulary. Did you know that many English words originate from Arabic? for e.g.

الكحول – Alcohol

سكر – sugar

الجبر – Algebra

صحراء – Sahara

قيثارة – Guitar

قطن – Cotton

and many more!

<u>Islam</u>

I STRONGLY advise you to study Arabic if you are a Muslim. Yes, the Quran and Hadith are available in English translation. Nonetheless, these translations are simply interpretations, and there are many gems and words/meanings that cannot be translated into English. (DONE)

For traveling purposes

Another compelling reason to learn Arabic is if you like travelling and learning about different cultures and traditions. This is because Arabic is the official language of twenty countries. You will get access and be able to communicate with individuals in these nations if you learn the language. You will get the opportunity to experience "Arab hospitality," which, in my opinion, is second to none.

The root system

Three and four letters make up a root of a verb, as I have already mentioned. If you know the origin and the different patterns around this root, you will understand words you have never heard before!

Chapter 2 – The correct way to learn Arabic as a non-native speaker

In the West, I've come across many institutes and organisations that teach the Arabic language incorrectly! You see, many of these organisations and institutes will teach you Arabic grammar and morphology right from the start. Don't get me wrong: in the Arabic language, they are required fields. Still, it makes little sense for a non-native speaker to begin with grammar and morphology when they have no prior knowledge of the language's lexicon. What good is it to know a tonne of technical grammatical rules if you can't even introduce yourself in Arabic or carry on a simple conversation?

Consider this: how did you pick up the English language? Did you study a lot of English grammar to improve your ability to speak, write, and understand the language? NO is the answer! Listening to your parents, instructors, and siblings speak English helped you learn the language by gradually picking up phrases, idioms, words, and sentences. This is also the proper technique in Arabic and any other language, for that matter. By gradually acquiring the vocabulary, hearing it used, and putting it into practice.

The famed three-volume Madinah texts taught at the Islamic University of Madinah are the most well-known series in the West (or one of them). What's important to note is that the author (Dr V. Abdur Rahim) wrote these books to help Saudi Arabian students (and students from other countries) who already have a strong foundation in the Arabic language. They weren't taught to pupils who didn't have much of a vocabulary, to begin with. These books are still taught today, but guess what? These three books represent only a tiny part of the Arabic curriculum taught at the Islamic University of Madinah; many more books are taught about which people are unaware.

I made the same error when I first started studying the Madinah trilogy, consisting of three books. Guess what? I was unable to read the bulk of the Arabic material that was offered to me at the conclusion of it, I could hardly compose a single phrase in Arabic, and I was overall annoyed and bewildered. I had spent a total of 16 months studying the Arabic language at that point, and I wish someone had directed me in the right direction at the time. These Madinah books have very few dialogues in them that you can actively practise, and they are largely made up of grammar and morphological rules, which is of little help to a complete novice. At the end of this chapter, I will show you some of the best curriculums to study in the Arabic language, for a complete beginner.

Grammar study in Arabic is unquestionably crucial because, without it, little can be communicated. Nothing can be communicated, though, if you don't have a vocabulary! Now, I'm not suggesting you shouldn't learn Arabic grammar; far from it. I'm implying that non-native speakers should concentrate first on the language itself, including verbs, nouns, expressions, and sentence structures, and get comfortable expressing themselves before delving deeper into grammar.

I'd like to draw your attention to Tim Ferris' book "The 4-Hour Body." He applies the Pareto principle, popularly known as the "80/20 rule," in this work. Tim claims that anybody can learn 2,500 words in order to attain conversational fluency in speaking and comprehending a language, giving them 95 per cent competence and understanding in any conversational environment. That's just around a quarter of the Arabic lexicon. It may appear to be a large number of words, but if we break it down for you, you'll need to learn

208 words every month, 52 words per week, and 7 words every day; that seems a lot more manageable, right? The fact is that anyone with a sincere desire to study Arabic can do it!

NOTE – these three stages are done simultaneously and not one after the other. I will explain this further.

Just to round it up for you. This is the PROVEN system for anybody to effectively learn the Arabic language:

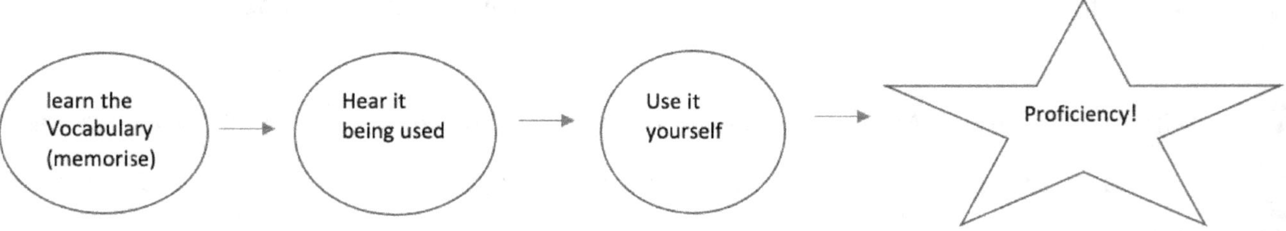

Now, let's break down each of these points a little more, so you can get some practical advice that can be implemented immediately!

Stage 1: Learn the Vocabulary

Finding the proper instructor to teach you a suitable curriculum is one of the most important aspects, even before you start learning Vocabulary. Depending on where you are in the globe, you may accomplish this in a variety of ways. Presume you live in the West (which I assume most of you do), i.e. the United Kingdom, the United States, and the majority of European nations. If such is the case, you have a number of alternatives. My first piece of advice is to look for a reliable Arabic language school in your neighbourhood. You may achieve this by conducting a social media search, a google search, or asking people who are well-known in the community to suggest you to someone who can help you.

However, given the current global COVID-19 epidemic, this is most certainly not a realistic choice for you. But don't fret; I've found a number of excellent Arabic learning colleges on the internet. Keep in mind that my suggestions are unbiased and based on my personal experience, as well as what I've read and heard from others. Also, keep in mind that these aren't the only solid choices available. These are the only ones with whom I have personal experience and can vouch for. If you do your homework, I'm sure you'll find a slew of other outstanding online Arabic language schools.

- Al Andalus Institute https://www.andalusinstitute.com/ - This is an excellent Arabic language programme lead by creator Muhammad al Andalusi, who takes you through the well-known Arabic language series "Al Arabiyyah bayna yadayk" over the course of 12-15 months. One of the reasons this course is so good is that Muhammad holds a weekly conversational session with his students (typically on

Saturday or Sunday) to assist them to talk and change from "cave language" to fluency and competency in as short as 12 months!

- Badr Academy London https://badracademy.co.uk/ - Badr Academy is a London-based institute that was founded in 2009. I personally know a few of the teachers at this institute, and I can testify for their teaching abilities and knowledge. This institute also provides one-on-one Quran lessons from Quran teachers who are highly skilled and knowledgeable in this discipline.

- Madinah College https://www.madinahcollege.uk/ – Unlike the other two institutes, Madinah College places a greater emphasis on Islamic studies rather than merely the Arabic language. They have an Alimiyyah course available (a programme designed to cover the fundamental science in Islam). That being said, they also provide excellent Arabic language tuition and are more affordable than the previous two institutes I listed.

- – Is there a free option? – Yes, you are correct. If you're on a limited budget, I've got a completely free alternative for you that you can begin right now from the comfort of your own home. The great series "Al Arabiyahh Bayna yadayk" has been covered by the Green lane Masjid YouTube channel, and the teacher, Ustadh Abdul Kareem, does a wonderful job breaking down the book and exercises from the very beginning – the link for this series is here:
https://www.youtube.com/watch?v=RTKlv_fUGvg&list=PL88CDD3C1F59C647D (

If you are a student who wants to go that extra mile and is serious about studying Arabic in a short amount of time, I would advise you to travel to the eastern area, particularly Egypt. That isn't to say that learning Arabic in other eastern nations isn't possible. It's just that I feel Egypt is the greatest option for the majority of people. Please allow me to explain why.

The cost...

Like most of the Middle East and Africa, living in Egypt is relatively affordable, especially if you are coming from the West, where the currency is much more stable. To be honest, it would take you a few months to save up enough money to travel to Egypt and study for 6-12 months (depending on where you want to live, your house/flat, and other expenditures), but it is unquestionably achievable and viable for most Western students. In Egypt, a trained instructor would cost around $1 per hour. (DONE)

The reputation...

Egypt has one of the best, if not the best, reputation for learning the Arabic language. Egypt is known to have some of the best Arabic learning institutes in the Arab world and worldwide. For e.g., Al Azhar University, Fajr Center, and Nile Arabic Center are some of the most well-regarded institutes and universities to study in, not mentioning possibly hundreds more. That is not all, you can even have your own 1 to 1 teacher if you want to, and you don't like the classroom settings.

The Accessibility…

This is a major reason why you should study in Egypt rather than elsewhere, and one that will save you a lot of trouble in the future. Obtaining a visa for Egypt is a simple process with minimal effort. However, if you wanted to study in another country, such as Saudi Arabia, you would need to apply for a student visa. That is, if you want to study at an Islamic University, but what if you don't want to devote the next four years to studying at one of those universities? Of course, you could come on a work visa, but it would be pointless, right? We are not here to work but to study. The final option is to go on an Umrah visa and then try to remain. However, this is not advised and might have severe ramifications and consequences. This isn't to imply that acquiring a visa in other countries is difficult, but the procedure for acquiring one in Egypt is by far the simplest I've seen, and from what I've heard from students who have studied there. That, together with everything else I've said, should have persuaded you that Egypt is the best option for you! (DONE)

Ok. but how do I memorize Vocabulary?

You may have made up your mind about where you want to learn Arabic. However, how do you memorize vocabulary?

Before I give you some tips and tricks for learning vocabulary, I want you to understand that this is not a hard and fast rule and that not everyone will benefit from the same methods. You'll have to try out different things to determine what works best for you. As a result, some of the more effective methods for memorizing Arabic vocabulary include:

Learning the words IN CONTEXT

This, in my opinion, is the finest approach to learn Arabic and other languages vocabulary. This is because memorising a Vocabulary list with no context or guidance is pointless. Allow me to give you an example. Prepositions are used to finish phrases and give them meaning in the English language. For example, you may say, "I'm heading **to** the store." In Arabic, we'd say "انا ذاهب الى الدُّكَان" Notice how we utilised prepositions in both languages to finish and make sense of the phrases. Because he didn't look at the context, a person who simply memorises words and then attempts to arrange them into phrases would struggle to form a proper sentence. Many verbs in Arabic will be followed by a preposition to complete a sentence, and we shall discuss prepositions shortly. It is recommended that a student learns no more than 20 words each day because this affects memory retention. Although, in the end, it is determined by your memory and the amount of effort and time you commit to memorising Vocabulary.

Foldable paper

Take a sheet of paper and fold it in half, then cut down the fold and line up the sheets neatly and staple the top. Next, what you want to do is write a list of Arabic words on the outside, leaving a space between each word. You will repeat this process on the inside, noting the meaning of each word in English. Gradually flick between the two, learning one word at a time. After you have finished learning one page, stick it on the wall, and then make another page. You'll need to look at what you've stuck on the wall throughout the day to ensure that what you have learned settles in your mind. After a while, the wall will be filled with vocabulary sheets. With this method, it is ideal to get a relative or friend to test you. They don't even need to know how to read Arabic, as you can transliterate the Arabic words into English.

STEP 1 – Fold in half the sheet of paper, note that I used a blank A4 sheet of paper, but it is recommended to use lined paper, to make things more organised.

Step 2 – Cut in half evenly the piece of paper.

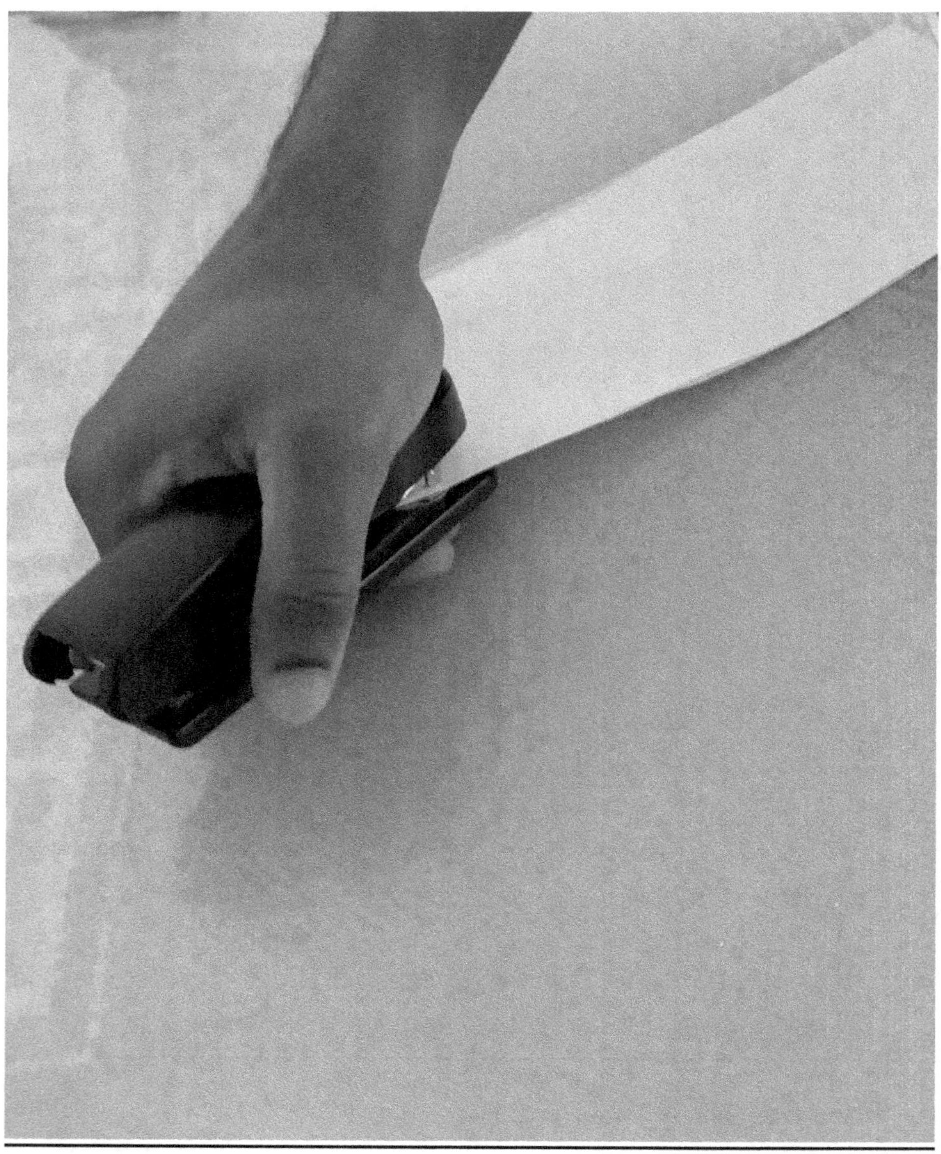

Step 3 – line the sheets neatly and staple the top.

Step 4 – Write a list of the Arabic vocabulary that you are tyring to memorise on the outside, leaving a small space in between each word.

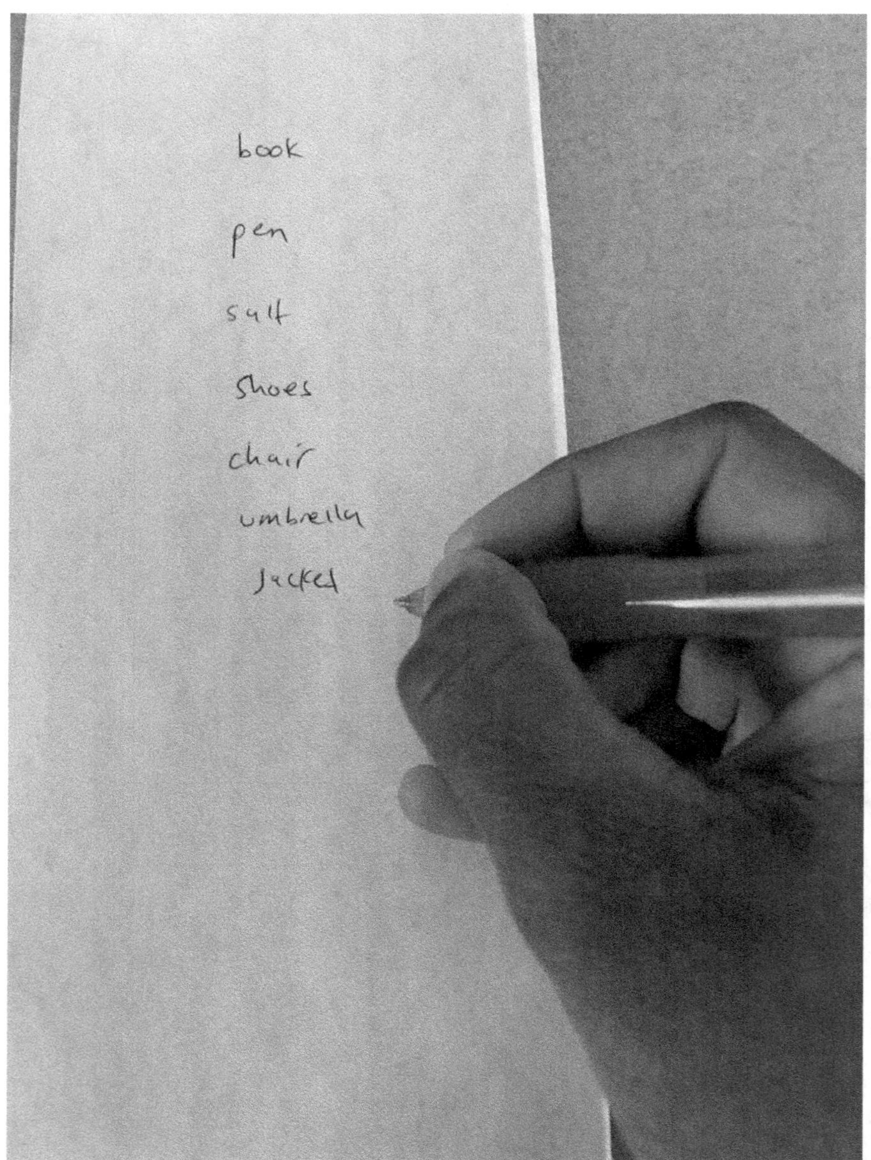

Step 5 – Write the translation of the Arabic words on the inside, then gradually flick through the two, learning one word at a time. I also recommend you to write a small sentence for each word (if you can) as that will most likely allow you to remember the word a lot easier (don't mind my crappy handwriting lol)

Step 6 - After a while, the wall will be filled with vocabulary sheets, and you would have learned a ton of vocabulary! this is the method that I personally used to learn vocabulary, I highly recommend you to also use this method, not only is it easy, but it is also very fun and fulfilling, to wake up everyday and see your progress infront of your eyes.

Flashcards

Flashcards are not a new concept, and they have shown to be effective for many students over the years. The flashcard would be two-sided, with the Arabic word on one side and the English translation on the other. The "Spaced repetition" strategy is one approach to make good use of flashcards. This strategy involves looking at your flashcards, leaving gaps, and then revisiting them. I recommend writing the Arabic term on one side of the flashcard and then using a sentence to define it on the other. Because you will use this term in a sentence, you are more likely to remember it. Over the course of a month, you will undoubtedly have acquired those Vocabulary in your long-term memory.

Memorise through selection

During the course of your Arabic language studies. You'll probably come across many texts and passages where there are a lot of terms you don't understand. The majority of individuals would underline all of the keywords they don't understand and then check up each word in the text. However, focusing just on the important words is a lot more effective method to achieve it. This is because the brain filters out a large number of words that it considers unimportant. As a result, you should concentrate on one-third of the words in the text, as the brain will remember those words if they are important.

Whatever way you choose to memorise Vocabulary, keep in mind that repetition is your best friend when it comes to storing knowledge in your long-term memory. Because we are all unique and store knowledge differently, the number of repetitions will vary from person to person. You will, however, need to devote some time to practising the Vocabulary. I would also advise you to conduct your revisions out loud rather than in your brain. This is because hearing yourself say the phrases can help you improve your pronunciation over time, especially because certain Arabic terms are difficult to pronounce even for native speakers!

Stage 2: Hear it being used

We are now at the 2nd stage of the three-stage Arabic language proficiency method. Bear in mind that you will be learning and memorizing Vocabulary and hearing it being used simultaneously. What do I mean by this?

The Arabic series that you have decided to study will come with some Audio CDs. Each chapter will have texts and exercises which can be listened to on a CD. For e.g., Al Arabiyyah bayna yadayk has audio sets which come with the book when you purchase. If, however you do not have those audio sets, they can be found online very quickly. However, this shouldn't be a problem for you anyway because you would have hopefully found a teacher by this stage. The teacher will guide you through the series of books. They will read out all the texts and exercises slowly so you can hear them and take it in slowly. After some time (I would say about 6-8 months), your Arabic language would have improved so much that now you would be ready to take it to a further step. At this stage, I would recommend you to start:

- Watching Arabic-language television (in modern standard Arabic, not any dialect) – I wouldn't recommend watching with subtitles. If you encounter unfamiliar words, phrases, or idioms, jot them down and look them up later. Again, in context.

- Watching Arabic news - This is an excellent method to improve your listening and comprehension skills. This is because the news is a location where all kinds of topics are covered, so you're broadening your vocabulary in various areas.

- Anime/Kids shows - as amusing as it may sound, this is a terrific approach to boost your knowledge and comprehension. This is due to the fact that these TV programmes were made in the purest version of Arabic to appeal to youngsters. There are no dialects in these shows since they wanted the youngsters to learn the standard Arabic language first.

Stage 3: Use it yourself

As you'll see, many individuals will be able to read high-quality Arabic literature with ease. They may be able to read practically any Arabic material and comprehend the bulk of it. However, you see that these people's speaking abilities are shaky. You might wonder why this is the case.

This is due to the fact that these individuals forgot to practise speaking the language while learning it. And this is something I want to be clear about right now. You don't start practising how to talk when you think you've accumulated a large vocabulary because if you do, you'll end up speaking in "cave language." Your statements will most likely be illogical, you will stutter frequently, and you will be extremely frustrated. You must practise speaking the language from the very beginning, beginning with the first pieces of vocabulary you acquire. This is so you may become accustomed to speaking the language early on and overcome the "broken language barrier."

If you have a teacher, request that they begin practising speaking with you as soon as possible. It may be difficult, and you may be ridiculed, but I guarantee you that the advantages will be enormous. From the beginning, you will be corrected on your speaking abilities. You'll be able to identify what you need to work on in order to talk more effectively and gracefully. You want to immerse yourself in the language as much as possible, so try to speak Arabic at home, with your siblings, and with your friends. This is the only method to develop your speaking skills.

What if I don't have somebody with whom to practise? This is a prevalent issue for people, particularly in the West, who do not have friends or family members who are proficient in Arabic. In this scenario, I can provide some advice.

- Try to incorporate the Arabic language in your daily life – before you say what you want to say in English, ask yourself if it's a sentence that could be said in Arabic. Say it even if you are muttering it to yourself.

- Write some short stories using the vocabulary that you've acquired over the course of this period. Get a notebook where you write some stories every week. No matter how basic the stories are that you are writing, if you do this consistently, you will not forget all of the Vocabulary that you have managed to learn, even though you are not speaking.

- Speaking is the best option, but if you cannot speak with anybody, then hearing the Arabic language in a recording (That could be an audiobook, a movie, the news) can be just as helpful.

To end this chapter, I want to recommend you some great Arabic language books/curriculums that you can study with a teacher/in a class, depending on your preferences.

- يديك بين العربية – This is the curriculum that I followed. In the former curriculum, there were four books; in the current curriculum, there are eight. This is an excellent series because it focuses mostly on conversational Arabic. Each chapter has a text with new vocabulary and verbs, as well as several activities for you to practise. Additionally, as previously stated, this course includes a CD audio set that allows you to listen to each activity independently and advance at your own pace. This series likewise progressively introduces you to the grammar, with only a small piece of it being presented in each chapter.

- للناشئين العربية – In terms of book layout, activities, and substance, this book is nearly identical to the first series. I haven't studied this series before, but I've heard fantastic things about it from individuals who have.

- الانبياء قصص - This is a single book, not a series. I recommend that you read this book once you have completed a whole curriculum. The book is centred on stories about the prophets, and it is intended for students who have completed a basic level of Arabic and wish to expand their vocabulary.

Note – These are the curriculums/books that I can personally recommend; nevertheless, this does not rule out the possibility of studying others. You might be wondering, "OK, how can I tell if a curriculum is the appropriate one to study as a beginner?" Observe the following guidelines:

- If it is bombarded with Grammar and morphology rules, avoid it.
- Go for one with basic conversations and short stories.
- Find a curriculum that has writing activities as that will give you plenty of practise.

After completing a series in Arabic, you should feel comfortable in 95 per cent of all conversational situations. I want to make it clear that this series of books will not teach you the language in its entirety. It should go without saying, but there is no book that can teach you all you need to know. These books will prepare you to enhance your knowledge of the Arabic language. The series will solely provide you with the tools you need to improve your Arabic language skills. It will also enable you to utilise an Arabic dictionary competently, allowing you to return at your leisure and obtain more advantage from different words/phrases. After completing an Arabic Language course, it is the student's responsibility to review what they have learnt and memorised on a regular basis. It is a language that is rapidly forgotten if it is not practised on a regular basis.

Chapter 3 – What if I can't read or write Arabic?

You see, this book was primarily made for those who had a small foundation in the Arabic Language. However, if you have read up until this point and you are a person who wants to learn the Arabic Language but you do not know how to read and write, I got you!

If you follow what I'm going to teach you, you may go from complete beginner to reading and writing Arabic in as little as 2-3 weeks. I'll make it as easy as possible for you by giving you everything you'll need to read and write. I am a firm believer in focusing on less but achieving more!

Stage 1: The Alphabet (Al-Huruuf)

Yes, we begin with the alphabet, just like we would with any other language we are attempting to learn. The number of letters in the Arabic language has been a point of contention. Some people believe it is 28, while others believe it is 29. Those that claim 28 do not include the letter ء in their total (Hamzaa). Let's assume there are 29 letters. With that out of the way, let's get started on the alphabet. I strongly suggest that you memorize the alphabet. It may seem daunting at first, but I assure you that you can master this in as little as 3-4 days. I'll start with the Arabic script and then transliterate it into English. Also, I strongly urge you to get the audiobook version of this book, as it will aid you with pronouncing the alphabet and what follows. Also, in Arabic, we start from the right-hand side, rather than the left, as we do in English. Therefore, the alphabet begins at the top right.

ج (Jeem)	ث (Thaa)	ت (Taa)	ب (Baa)	ا (Alif)
ر (Ra)	ذ (Dhaal)	د (Daal)	خ (Khaa)	ح (Haa)
ض (Daad)	ص (Saad)	ش (Sheen)	س (Seen)	ز (Zayn)
ف (Fa)	غ (Gayn)	ع (Ayn)	ظ (Thaa)	ط (Taah)
ن (Noon)	م (Meem)	ل (laam)	ك (Kaaf)	ق (Qaaf)
	ي (Yaa)	ء (Hamza)	و (Waw)	ه (Haa)

- **Step 1** – Find a quiet place in your house where there are no distractions.
- **Step 2** - Listen to the audiobook while you are following the letters with your eyes.
- **Step 3** – After you have finished the alphabet, take at least a 30 - 2 hours break, do something completely different.
- **Step 4** – after the rest, come back and repeat the whole alphabet 50 times, without the audio set this time. This time though, do not focus on the English transliteration and focus on the Arabic only.
- **Step 5** – Do 25 repetitions looking at the alphabet, and then attempt to do another 25 by heart.
- **If you follow all of these steps, you should be able to memorise the alphabet in 2-4 days in total.**

Stage 2: The vowelization of the letters (Al-Harakaat)

حَرَكَةُ الضَّمَّة (This is an Ooo sound)	حَرَكَةُ الكَسْرَة (This is an Eee sound)	حَرَكَةُ الفَتْحَة (This is an Aaa sound)
أُ بُ تُ	إِ بِ تِ	أَ بَ تَ
أُ جُ حُ	إِ جِ حِ	أَ جَ حَ
خُ دُ ذُ	خِ دِ ذِ	خَ دَ ذَ
رُ زُ سُ	رِ زِ سِ	رَ زَ سَ
شُ صُ ضُ	شِ صِ ضِ	شَ صَ ضَ
طُ ظُ عُ	طِ ظِ عِ	طَ ظَ عَ
غُ فُ قُ	غِ فِ قِ	غَ فَ قَ
كُ لُ مُ	كِ لِ مِ	كَ لَ مَ
نُ هُ وُ	نِ هِ وِ	نَ هَ وَ
	يَ يِ يُ	

These are the vowels that make the different sounds for the letters. We will focus on all three of them. They are Al fathah, Al Dammah and al Kasrah. Follow the table below.

- **Step 1** – Focus carefully on the three vowel sounds, go through each and everyone slowly.

- **Step 2** - Listen to the Audiobook and follow along simultaneously

- **Step 3** - After you have become fluent with the vowels, attempt the following exercise below.

نَشِطَ	بَرِئَ	طَمَخَ
ضَحِكَ	مَرِحَ	أَذِنَ
دَسِمَ	رَكِبَ	مَرَجَ
خَجِلَ	دَكِنَ	شَتِمَ
عَنِتَ	صَحِبَ	جَنِفَ
دَهِشَ	لَغِبَ	بَرِقَ
وَزِرَ	هَلَعَ	دَلِهَ
قَضِمَ	كَئِبَ	نَغِصَ

Stage 3: The prolongation of letters

The letters of prolongation, which is known in Arabic as "Huruuf al Madd" are three, they are:

- مد بِالأَلِف – Prolongation with the letter Alif

- مد بِاليَاء – Prolongation with the letter ya

- مد بِالوَاو – Prolongation with the letter waaw

These three letters give a small prolongation when they come with a letter. The below table will illustrate this. Note that the letters in red mean the words have now been elongated for roughly another second. The letters in red are the last letters.

مد بِالوَاو	مد بِالياء	مد بِالأَلِف
أُ . أُو	إ . إي	ء . ءآ
بُ . بُو	بِ . بِ ي	بَ . بآ
ثُ . ثُو	تِ . تِ ي	تَ . تَا
ثُ . ثُو	ثَ . ثِ ي	ثَ . ثَا
جُ . جُو	جِ . جِ ي	جَ . جَا
حُ . حُو	حِ . حِ ي	حَ . حَا
خُ . خُو	خِ . خِ ي	خَ . خَا
دُ . دُو	دِ . دِي	دَ . دَا
ذُ . ذُو	ذِ . ذِي	ذَ . ذَا
رُ . رُو	رِ . رِي	رَ . رَا

Prolongation of the letter "Alif"

قَامَ — Now it becomes Qaama.	قَمَ - You will now stretch it with the addition of an Alif.
بَالَ — Now it becomes Baala.	بَلَ — You will now stretch it with the addition of an Alif.
فَاقَ — Now it becomes Faaqa.	فَقَ — You will now stretch it with the addition of an Alif.

Prolongation of the letter "Ya"

قِيلَ — Now it becomes Qeela.	قِلَ — You will now stretch it with the addition of the Yaa.
رِيحَ — Now it becomes Reeha.	رِحَ — You will now stretch it with the addition of the Yaa.
مِيدَ — Now it becomes Meeda.	مِدَ — You will now stretch it with the addition of the Yaa.

Prolongation of the letter "Waaw"

غُرُوبٌ – Now it becomes Quruwwbun.	غَرْبٌ – You will now stretch it with the addition of the Waaw.
يُوعَظُ – Now it becomes Yuwwazoo.	وَعَظُ – You will now stretch it with the addition of the Waaw.
دَخَلُوهُ – Now it becomes dagaluuhu.	دَخَلَ – You will now stretch it with the addition of the Waaw.

The concept itself is very simple and requires little practice until you get the hang of the prolongation. Note that the prolongation should only be a slight prolongation and not a long one.

Stage 4 – The silent (Sukoon)

The Sukoon is mandatory for everybody to learn. It is a silent vowel in the word. It looks like a small circle, and you will see it at the top of a word. What it does is that it silences the letter. Below I will give you some examples of the sukoon for you to be able to grasp this concept. I have highlighted the letter that has the sukoon on it to make it easier for you to recognize. Note that the letter with sukoon has a small "o" at the top of the letter.

أُخْت	أَبْ	قُلْ
نَمْ	ذُقْ	مُتْ
قُمْ	قِفْ	خُذْ
مُنْذُ	فَوْقَ	تَحْتَ
نَوْمَ	شَوْقَ	مَوْتَ
يَوْمَ	كَيْلَ	مَيْلَ
فَجْرَ	قُرْبَ	بَعْضَ
حُسْنُ	عُمْرُ	شَوْطُ

Notice how we are silencing the letter with the sukoon on it. We do not pronounce it as we do with the other vowels. Again, make sure you are following along with the audiobook to know how to pronounce the silent vowel.

Stage 5 – The double vowel (Tanween)

The double vowel, which is known as التَّنْوِين in Arabic, is basically the sound of a noon at the end of a word, yet the noon itself is not written. You have the double vowel (Al Tanween) of the fathah, the kasrah, and the dammah. Let's begin with tanween al fathah.

تَنْوِين الفَتْحَتَين

شَنْ – شأً   دَنْ– دأً   بَنْ– بأً

The reason why we call it this is because you will see two fathas, two lines at the top of the last word, which will make the sound of a noon. To benefit from and understand this concept, I highly advise you to follow along with the audiobook, as it would otherwise be very difficult to understand as a complete beginner.

Note – as you can see, when you pronounce the word with tanween, you get a noon sound in the end. However, I want to clarify that these noons are not written when you want to write in tanween. This was only used to demonstrate the similarities in pronunciation and to help you understand the concept. Now, let us look at an exercise for fathah tanween. Again, I have highlighted the letter of tanween in red. The letter of Tanween is the last letter.

كِتَاباً	لاعِباً	أَبَداً
سَرِيراً	قَرِيباً	قَمَراً
سَرْمَداً	نَهَاراً	قِيَماً
شَرْقاً	غَرْباً	جَنُوباً
مَعْرُوضاً	مَكْتُوباً	حَافِظاً

تَنْوين الكَسْرَتَين

This is, again, the same concept, but this time we are applying it to al kasrah.

صِنْ - صٍ	يِنْ . يٍ	طِنْ . طٍ

لُوطٍ	أعْمَالٍ	جُنُبٍ
مِفْتَاح	سُلْطَانٍ	شَعَبٍ
بَيْتٍ	حَامِلٍ	أَدَبٍ
شَاكِرٍ	حَفِيظٍ	سَلِيمٍ
مُحِيطٍ	أَلِيمٍ	مَلَكٍ

Again, I highly advise you to follow along with the audiobook to benefit from the activity.

تَنْوِين الضَّمَّتَين

جُنْ - جٌّ	رُنْ - رٌّ	وُنْ - وٌّ

Again, the same concept applies to al dammah. Carefully follow along with the audiobook.

إيمَانٌ	مَاهِرٌ	كِتَابٌ
بَرْقٌ	ثَلْجٌ	ظُلْمٌ
نَخْلٌ	عَرْشٌ	شَمْسٌ
ثَوْبٌ	لِبَاسٌ	وَجْهٌ
سَاجِدٌ	مَوْلُودٌ	مِلْحٌ

Stage 6: The double vowel (Al shadda)

The "Shadda" is the last vowel which we will go over. Knowing the shadda fluently is very important, as it is higly prevalent in the Arabic language and crucial for you to read efficiently. In simpler terms, the shadda Is two of the same letters merged into one, but only one letter is written, and you will see a small "W" at the top of the letter.

مَدْدَ - مَدَّ   شَدْدَ - شَدَّ   صَنْنَ - صَنَّ

As you can see with the first example, when there is a shadda on a letter, it sounds like

مَنَّ	رَدَّ	سَدَّ
كَنَّ	رَسَّ	بَنَّ
حَقَّقَ	شَيَّدَ	زَيَّنَ
بَدَّلَ	صَنَّفَ	وَقَّفَ
قَتَّلَ	سَمَّنَ	رَكَّبَ

there is one letter that is silent before it, and one that has a fathah, together when you combine them, you get the shadda sign, and you drop one of the letters. Carefully follow along with the audiobook the following exercise.

Stage 7: Putting it all together!

If you've made it this far, you're almost there! It's time to put everything together and start writing in Arabic. Writing gets quite simple as long as you can distinguish words and letters and have them in your head. Try to write down everything you can, every phrase, verb, and expression you come across. I strongly advise you to write it down so you can become accustomed to writing. I recommend that you copy out the verb conjugations since this will greatly improve your Arabic writing skills.

Chapter 4 – The 100 Arabic verbs any beginner MUST know!

Let's have a look at the 100 Arabic verbs that every beginner should know. I'll give you the verb and all of its conjugations. I'll next give you all of the verb's various translations, as well as three examples for each verb to demonstrate how to use it in a sentence. I've included a little verb guide below; please read it fully and comprehend it before moving on to the verbs so that you don't become overwhelmed by the phrases you'll encounter.

Verb conjuation Guide

- هُوَ – Masculine singular in 3rd person, in English the pronoun would be "he."

- هُمَا – Masculine dual in 3rd person, "they" (2 males).

- هُمْ – Masculine plural in 3rd person, "they" (3+ males).

- هِيَ – Feminine singular in 3rd person, in English the pronoun would be "she."

- هُمَا – Feminine dual in 3rd person, "they" (2 females).

- هُنَّ – Feminine plural in 3rd person, "they" (3+ females).

- أَنْتَ — Masculine singular in 2nd person, the English pronoun would be "you" (1 male).

- أَنْتُمَا — Masculine dual in 2nd person, "you" (2 males).

- أَنْتُمْ — Masculine plural in 2nd person, "you" (3+ males).

- أَنْتِ –Feminine singular in 2nd person, the English pronoun would be "you" (1 female).

- أَنْتُمَا — Feminine dual in 2nd person, "you" (2 females).

- أَنْتُنَّ – Female plural in 2nd person, "you" (3+ females).

- أَنَا – Masculine + feminine 1st person singular, "I."

- نَحْنُ – Masculine + feminine 1st person plural, "we" (3+).

- الْمَصْدَر – The verbal noun, in simpler terms, is the" i-n-g" version of the verb. For e.g., for the first verb, that would be the act of "looking," "considering," or "reviewing," depending on the context in which it is used.

- اِسْم الْفَاعِل – An active particle, in simpler terms, is the person doing the verb. Again, for the first verb, the active particle would be the "looker," "the considerer," or the "reviewer" depending on the context – note that the action can be ongoing or completed, as long as it's in the "Active voice."

- اِسْم الْمَفْعُول – The passive particle, in simpler terms, is the thing upon which the action is done. For e.g., for the first verb, the passive article is "the thing being looked at," or "the thing being considered" or "the thing being reviewed," depending on the context.

Arabic conjugation is not as complex as some people make it out to be. If you carefully follow my guide, you will master the conjugation of verbs within no time. Also, there is no need to memorize the conjugation of verbs. Once you practice it a couple of times, you will get the hang of it. This is because you will realize that it follows the same pattern every time. This is very useful because when you decide to further your studies in the Arabic language and discover more and more verbs, you will be able to quickly conjugate them, just by having the root of the verb, i.e., masculine singular, in 3rd person "he." However, it is advisable to memorize the order of the pronouns, as you will find that it will help you a lot going forward. To make things easier for you. I will go through the first two verbs with you to get a good grip of them. I recommend you to make a note of any words/verbs that you do not understand in a separate notebook and re-write the sentences to improve your writing

Verb #1 – نَظَرَ – he looked, he considered, he reviewed (comes with إلى)

إِسْم الْمَفْعُول (The passive participle)	إِسْم الْفَاعِل (The active participle)	الْمَصْدَر (Verbal Noun)	أَمْر (Imperative)	الْمُضَارِع (Present)	الْمَاضِي (Past)	الضَّمِير (pronoun)
مَنْظُور	نَاظِر	نَظَر		يَنْظُر / يَنْظُرَانِ / يَنْظُرُونَ	نَظَرَ / نَظَرَا / نَظَرُوا	هُوَ / هُمَا / هُمْ
				تَنْظُر / تَنْظُرَانِ / يَنْظُرْنَ	نَظَرَتْ / نَظَرَتَا / نَظَرْنَ	هِيَ / هُمَا / هُنَّ
			أُنْظُرْ / أُنْظُرَا / أُنْظُرُوا	تَنْظُر / تَنْظُرَان / تَنْظُرُون	نَظَرْتَ / نظرتما / نَظَرْتُمْ	أَنْتَ / أَنْتُمَا / أَنْتُمْ
			أُنْظُرِي / أُنْظُرَا / أُنْظُرْنَ	تَنْظُرِينَ / تَنْظُرَان / يَنْظُرْنَ	نَظَرْتِ / نظرتما / نَظَرْنَ	أَنْتِ / أَنْتُمَا / أَنْتُنَّ
				أَنْظُر / نَنْظُر	نَظَرْتُ / نَظَرْنَا	أَنَا / نَحْنُ

Verb #1 conjuation help!

هُوَ — he looked. (1 male)	هِيَ — she looked (1 female)
هُمَا — they looked (2 males)	هُمَا — they looked (2 females)
هُمْ — they looked (3+ males)	هُنَّ — they looked (3+ females)

أَنْتَ — you looked (1 male)	أَنْتِ — you looked (1 female)
أَنْتُمَا — you looked (2 males)	أَنْتُمَا — you looked (2 females)
أَنْتُمْ — you looked (3+ males)	أَنْتُنَّ — you looked (3+ females)

أَنَا — I looked, both male and female
نَحْنُ — we looked, both male and female

اِسْم الْفَاعِل — this is the doer of the action, that would be the "looker" or the" reviewer" or the "considered" depending on the context

اِسْم الْمَفْعُول — this would be "the theing being looked at" or "the thing being reviewed" or "the thing being considered" depending on the context

الْمَصْدَر — so this would be "looking" "reviewing" or "considering" depening on the context.

Sentences

لِمَ تَنْظُرُ إِلَيَّ يَا خالد ؟ .1

أَحْتَاجُكَ انْ تُعِيدَ النَّظَرَ إِلى أُسْلُوبِكَ .2

سَأَنْظُرُ فِي الأمر .3

English translation

1. Why are you looking at me, khalid?
2. I need you to review your behaviour/ways.
3. I will consider it.

Verb #2 – سَمِعَ – To hear

اِسْم الْمَفْعُول (The passive participle)	اِسْم الْفَاعِل (The active participle)	الْمَصْدَر (Verbal Noun)	أَمْرّ (Imperative)	الْمُضَارع (Present)	الْمَاضِى (Past)	الضَّمِير (pronoun)
مَسْمُوع	سَامِع	سَمْع		يَسْمَعُ / يَسْمَعَان / يَسْمَعُونَ	سَمِعَ / سَمِعَا / سَمِعُوا	هُوَ / هُمَا / هُمْ
				تَسْمَعُ / تَسْمَعَان / يَسْمَعْنَ	سَمِعَتْ / سَمِعَتَا / سَمِعْنَ	هِيَ / هُمَا / هُنَّ
			اِسْمَعْ / اِسْمَعَا / اِسْمَعُوا	تَسْمَعُ / تَسْمَعَا / تَسْمَعُونَ	سَمِعْتَ / سَمِعْتُمَا / سَمِعْتُمْ	أَنْتَ / أَنْتُمَا / أَنْتُمْ
			اِسْمَعِى / اِسْمَعَا / اِسْمَعْنَ	تَسْمَعِينَ / تَسْمَعَا / تَسْمَعْنَ	سَمِعْتِ / سَمِعْتُمَا / سَمِعْتُنَّ	أَنْتِ / أَنْتُمَا / أَنْتُنَّ
				أَسْمَعُ / نَسْمَعُ	سَمِعْتُ / سَمِعْنَا	أَنَا / نَحْنُ

Verb #2 conjuation help!

هُوَ — he heard (1 male)	هِيَ — she heard (1 female)
هُمَا — they heard (2 males)	هُمَا — they heard (2 females)
هُمْ — they heard (3+ males)	هُنَّ — they heard (3+ females)

أَنْتَ — you heard (1 male)	أَنْتِ — you heard (1 female)
أَنْتُمَا — you heard (2 males)	أَنْتُمَا — you heard (2 females)
أَنْتُمْ — you looked (3+ males)	أَنْتُنَّ — you heard (3+ females)

أَنَا — I heard, both male and female
نَحْنُ — we heard, both male and female

اِسْم الْفَاعِل — this is the doer of the action, that would be the "hearer"

اِسْم الْمَفْعُول — this would be "the thing that is heard"

الْمَصْدَر - this would be the act of "hearing"

Sentences

1. سَمِعتُ أَنَك مُتَزَّوجٌ
2. سَمِعَ خَالِدُ الْقُرْآنَ
3. الْقُدْرَةُ عَلى السَمع نِعْمَةٌ

English translation

1. I heard that you are married.
2. Khalid heard the Quran.
3. Having the ability to hear is a blessing.

Verb #3 – أَعَادَ – to return, to restore

اِسْم الْمَفْعُول (The passive participle)	اِسْم الْفَاعِل (The active participle)	الْمَصْدَر (Verbal Noun)	أَمْر (Imperative)	الْمُضَارِع (Present)	الْمَاضِي (Past)	الضَّمِير (Pronoun)
مُعَاد	مُعِيد	إِعَادَة		يُعِيدُ يُعِيدَانِ يُعِيدُونَ	أَعَادَ أَعَادَا أَعَادُوا	هُوَ هُمَا هُمْ
				تُعِيدُ تُعِيدَانِ يُعِدْنَ	أَعَادَتْ أَعَادَتَا أَعَدْنَ	هِيَ هُمَا هُنَّ
			أَعِدْ أَعِيدَا أَعِيدُوا	تُعِيدُ تُعِيدَانِ تُعِيدُوا	أَعَدْتَ أَعَدْتُمَا أَعَدْتُمْ	أَنْتَ أَنْتُمَا أَنْتُمْ
			أَعِيدِي أَعِيدَا أَعِدْنَ	تُعِيدِينَ تُعِيدَانِ تُعِدْنَ	أَعَدْتِ أَعَدْتُمَا أَعَدْتُنَّ	أَنْتِ أَنْتُمَا أَنْتُنَّ
				أُعِيدُ نُعِيدُ	أَعَدْتُ أَعَدْنَا	أَنَا نَحْنُ

<u>Sentences</u>

1. أَعَدْتُ اِلى البَيتِ بَعْدَ المَدْرَسَةِ
2. لَمَ يُعِيدْ الْمَطَارُ جَوَازَ سَفَري
3. أَعَادَ الرَجُلُ اِلى الرِّيَاضَةِ بَعْدَ فَتْرَةٍ مِن الْإِجَازَةِ

<u>English translation</u>

1. I returned home after school.
2. The airport didn't return my passport.
3.The man returned to sports after a while off.

Verb #4 – أَشَارَ – to point, indicate, refer

اِسْم الْمَفْعُول (The passive participle)	اِسْم الْفَاعِل (The active participle)	الْمَصْدَر (Verbal Noun)	أَمْر (Imperative)	الْمُضَارِع (Present)	الْمَاضِي (Past)	الضَّمِير (pronoun)
مُشَار	مُشِير	إِشَارَة		يُشِيرُ / يُشِيرَانِ / يُشِيرُونَ	أَشَارَ / أَشَارَا / أَشَارُوا	هُوَ / هُمَا / هُمْ
				تُشِيرُ / تُشِيرَانِ / يُشِرْنَ	أَشَارَتْ / أَشَارَتَا / أَشَرْنَ	هِيَ / هُمَا / هُنَّ
			أَشِرْ / أَشِيرَا / أَشِيرُوا	تُشِيرُ / تُشِيرَانِ / تُشِيرُونَ	أَشَرْتَ / أَشَرْتُمَا / أَشَرْتُمْ	أَنْتَ / أَنْتُمَا / أَنْتُمْ
			أَشِيرِي / أَشِيرَا / أَشِرْنَ	تُشِيرِينَ / تُشِيرَانِ / تُشِرْنَ	أَشَرْتِ / أَشَرْتُمَا / أَشَرْتُنَّ	أَنْتِ / أَنْتُمَا / أَنْتُنَّ
				أُشِيرُ / نُشِيرُ	أَشَرْتُ / أَشَرْنَا	أَنَا / نَحْنُ

Sentences

1. أَشَارَ الرَجُلُ إِلى أَخِيهِ

2. لا تُشِيرْ إِلى النَّاسِ

3. أَشَارَ المُدِيرُ إِلَيَّ في خِطَابِهِ

4. أَشَارَتْ الِامْرَأةُ يَمِيناً عِنْدَ إِشَارَاتِ الْمُرُورِ

English translation

1. The man pointed towards his prother.
2. Do not point at the people.
3. The head-teacher referred to me in his speech/He pointed to me.
4. The women indicated right at the traffic lights.

Verb #5 – وَضَعَ – To put, to establish, to set up

اِسْم الْمَفْعُول (The passive participle)	اِسْم الْفَاعِل (The active participle)	الْمَصْدَر (Verbal Noun)	أَمْر (Imperative)	الْمُضَارِع (Present)	الْمَاضِى (Past)	الضّمِير (pronoun)
مَوْضُوع	وَاضِع	وَضْع		يَضَعُ / يَضَعَانِ / يَضَعُونَ	وَضَعَ / وَضَعَا / وَضَعُوا	هُوَ / هُمَا / هُمْ
				تَضَعُ / تَضَعَانِ / يَضَعْنَ	وَضَعَتْ / وَضَعَتَا / وَضَعْنَ	هِيَ / هُمَا / هُنَّ
			ضَعْ / ضَعَا / ضَعُوا	تَضَعُ / تَضَعَانِ / تَضَعُونَ	وَضَعْتَ / وَضَعْتُمَا / وَضَعْتُمْ	أَنْتَ / أَنْتُمَا / أَنْتُمْ
			ضَعِي / ضَعَا / ضَعْنَ	تَضَعِينَ / تَضَعَانِ / تَضَعْنَ	وَضَعْتِ / وَضَعْتُمَا / وَضَعْتُنَّ	أَنْتِ / أَنْتُمَا / أَنْتُنَّ
				أَضَعُ / نَضَعُ	وَضَعْتُ / وَضَعْنَا	أَنَا / نَحْنُ

Sentences

1. وَضَعَ الوَلَدُ المَحْمُوْلَ على المَائِدةِ.
2. وَضَعَتِ المُنَظَّمَةُ مَكَانً لِلرَاحَةِ.
3. لا تَضَعْ يَدَكَ هُنَاكَ.

English translation

1. The boy put the laptop on the table.
2. The oranisation established a resting place.
3. Do not place your hands there.

Verb #6 – قَالَ – To Say

اِسْم الْمَفْعُول (The passive participle)	اِسْم الْفَاعِل (The active participle)	الْمَصْدَر (Verbal Noun)	أَمْرٌ (Imperative)	الْمُضَارِع (Present)	الْمَاضِي (Past)	الضَّمِير (pronoun)
مَقُول	قَائِل	قَوْل		يَقُولُ يَقُولَانِ يَقُولُونَ	قَالَ قَالَا قَالُوا	هُوَ هُمَا هُمْ
				تَقُولُ تَقُولَانِ يَقُلْنَ	قَالَتْ قَالَتَا قُلْنَ	هِيَ هُمَا هُنَّ
			قُلْ قُولَا قُولُوا	تَقُولُ تَقُولَانِ تَقُولُونَ	قُلْتَ قُلْتُمَا قُلْتُمْ	أَنْتَ أَنْتُمَا أَنْتُمْ
			قُولِي قُولَا قُلْنَ	تَقُولِينَ تَقُولَانِ تَقُلْنَ	قُلْتِ قُلْتُمَا قُلْتُنَّ	أَنْتِ أَنْتُمَا أَنْتُنَّ
				أَقُولُ نَقُولُ	قُلْتُ قُلْنَا	أَنَا نَحْنُ

Sentences

1. قَالَتْ مَرْيَمُ أَنّها غَضْبَانَةٌ

2. لا تَقُولْ قَوْلً غَيْرَ صَحِيح

3. قُلْتَ ذالك الأُسْبُوع المَاضِي

English translation

1. Mary said that she was angry.
2. Do not say a speech that is wrong.
3. You said that last week.

Verb #7 – سَأَلَ – To ask

اِسْم الْمَفْعُول (The passive participle)	اِسْم الْفَاعِل (The active participle)	الْمَصْدَر (Verbal Noun)	أمّر (Imperative)	الْمُضَارِع (Present)	الْمَاضِى (Past)	الضّمِير (pronoun)
مَسْؤُول	سَائِل	سُؤَال		يَسْأَلُ يَسْأَلَانِ يَسْأَلُونَ	سَأَلَ سَأَلَا سَأَلُوا	هُوَ هُمَا هُمْ
				تَسْأَلُ تَسْأَلَانِ يَسْأَلْنَ	سَأَلَتْ سَأَلَتَا سَأَلْنَ	هِيَ هُمَا هُنَّ
			اِسْأَلْ اِسْأَلَا اِسْأَلُوا	تَسْأَلُ تَسْأَلَانِ تَسْأَلُونَ	سَأَلْتَ سَأَلْتُمَا سَأَلْتُمْ	أنتَ أنتُمَا أنتُمْ
			اِسْأَلِي اِسْأَلَا اِسْأَلْنَ	تَسْأَلِينَ تَسْأَلَانِ تَسْأَلْنَ	سَأَلْتِ سَأَلْتُمَا سَأَلْتُنَّ	أنتِ أنتُمَا أنتُنَّ
				أسْأَلُ نَسْأَلُ	سَأَلْتُ سَأَلْنَا	أنَا نَحْنُ

Sentences

١. سَأَلَ عَنِّى المُدَرِّسُ فِى المَدْرَسَةِ
٢. لا تَسْأَلْنِى عَنْ هَذَا الامر
٣. مِن المُهِمِّ أَنْ تَطْرَحَ أَسْئِلَةً فِى الفَصْلِ

English translation

1. The teacher at the school asked about me.
2. Do not ask me concerning this matter.
3. It is important to ask questions in the classroom.

Verb #8 – قَرَأَ – to read, to recite, to review/study

اِسْم الْمَفْعُول (The passive participle)	اِسْم الْفَاعِل (The active participle)	الْمَصْدَر (Verbal Noun)	أَمْرٌ (Imperative)	الْمُضَارِع (Present)	الْمَاضِى (Past)	الضَّمِير (pronoun)
مَقْرُوء	قَارِئ	قِرَاءَة		يَقْرَأُ يَقْرَآنِ يَقْرَأُونَ	قَرَأَ قَرَآ قَرَأُوا	هُوَ هُمَا هُمْ
				تَقْرَأُ تَقْرَآنِ يَقْرَأْنَ	قَرَأَتْ قَرَأَتَا قَرَأْنَ	هِيَ هُمَا هُنَّ
			اِقْرَأْ اِقْرَآ اِقْرَأُوا	تَقْرَأُ تَقْرَآنِ تَقْرَأُونَ	قَرَأْتَ قَرَأْتُمَا قَرَأْتُمْ	أَنْتَ أَنْتُمَا أَنْتُمْ
			اِقْرَئِي اِقْرَآ اِقْرَأْنَ	تَقْرَئِينَ تَقْرَآنِ تَقْرَأْنَ	قَرَأْتِ قَرَأْتُمَا قَرَأْتُنَّ	أَنْتِ أَنْتُمَا أَنْتُنَّ
				أَقْرَأُ نَقْرَأُ	قَرَأْتُ قَرَأْنَا	أَنَا نَحْنُ

Sentences

1. أَحِبُّ قِرَاَةَ القُرْانِ

2. لا بُدَّ انْ تَقرأ الكُتُبَ كَثِيراً

3. قَرَأْتْ كَثِيرً مِن الصُحُفِ

English translation

1. I like reading the Quran
2. It is important that you read the books repeatedly.
3. She read many of the newspapers.

Verb #9 – أَجَابَ – to answer, to reply, to respond

اِسْم الْمَفْعُول (The passive participle)	اِسْم الْفَاعِل (The active participle)	الْمَصْدَر (Verbal Noun)	أَمْرُ (Imperative)	الْمُضَارِع (Present)	الْمَاضِي (Past)	الضَّمِير (pronoun)
مُجِيب	مُجَاب	إِجَابة		يُجِيب أُجِيبَا يُجِيبُونَ	أَجَاب يُجِيبَا أَجَابُوا	هُوَ هُمَا هُمْ
				تُجِيب تُجِيبَان يُجِبْنَ	أَجَابَتْ أَجَابَتَا أَجَبْنَ	هِيَ هُمَا هُنَّ
			أَجِبْ أَجِيبَا أَجِيبُوا	تُجِيب تُجِيبَان تُجِيبُونَ	أَجَبْتَ أَجَبْتُمَا أَجَبْتُمْ	أَنْتَ أَنْتُمَا أَنْتُمْ
			أَجِيبِي أَجِيبَا أَجِبْنَ	تُجِيبِينَ تُجِيبَان تُجِبْنَ	أَجَبْتِ أَجَبْتُمَا أَجَبْتُنَّ	أَنْتِ أَنْتُمَا أَنْتُنَّ
				أُجِيب نُجِيب	أَجَبْتُ أَجَبْنَا	أَنَا نَحْنُ

<u>Sentences</u>

١. مَا الإجابَةُ لِلأَسْئِلَةِ؟

٢. أَجَابَ الرَجُلُ إِلى السُؤَالِ

٣. أَجِبْ بِطَرِيقةٍ مُحْتَرِمةٍ لِوالِدَيْكَ

<u>English translation</u>

1. What is the answer to the question?
2. The man answered the question.
3. Respond to your parents in a respectful manner.

Verb #10 - مَرَّ – to pass by (comes with بِ)

اِسْم الْمَفْعُول (The passive participle)	اِسْم الْفَاعِل (The active participle)	الْمَصْدَر (Verbal Noun)	أَمْرٌ (Imperative)	الْمُضَارِع (Present)	الْمَاضِي (Past)	الضَّمِير (Pronoun)
مَمْرُور	مَارّ	مُرُور		يَمُرُّ / يَمُرَّانِ / يَمُرُّونَ	مَرَّ / مَرَّا / مَرُّوا	هُوَ / هُمَا / هُمْ
				تَمُرُّ / تَمُرَّانِ / يَمُرْنَ	مَرَّتْ / مَرَّتَا / مَرَرْنَ	هِيَ / هُمَا / هُنَّ
			مُرَّ / مُرَّا / مُرُّوا	تَمُرُّ / تَمُرَّانِ / تَمُرُّونَ	مَرَرْتَ / مَرَرْتُمَا / مَرَرْتُمْ	أَنْتَ / أَنْتُمَا / أَنْتُمْ
			مُرِّي / مُرَّا / أُمْرُرْنَ	تَمُرِّينَ / تَمُرَّانِ / تَمُرُرْنَ	مَرَرْتِ / مَرَرْتُمَا / مَرَرْتُنَّ	أَنْتِ / أَنْتُمَا / أَنْتُنَّ
				أَمُرُّ / نَمُرُّ	مَرَرْتُ / مَرَرْنَا	أَنَا / نَحْنُ

Sentences

١. مَرَرْتُ بِالمَدْرَسَةِ البَارِحَة

٢. هَلْ مَرَرْتِ بِالحَافِلَةِ اليَوْمَ؟

٣. مَرَّ بِالمُسْتَشْفَى أَحْمَد يَوْمَ الخَمِيس

English translation

1. I passed by the school yesterday.
2. Did you pass by the bus today?
3. Ahmed passed by the hospital on Thursday.

Verb #11 – نَسَخَ – to copy, to Abrogate

اِسْم الْمَفْعُول (The passive participle)	اِسْم الْفَاعِل (The active participle)	الْمَصْدَر (Verbal Noun)	أَمْرٌ (Imperative)	الْمُضَارِع (Present)	الْمَاضِي (Past)	الضَّمِير (pronoun)
مَنْسُوخ	نَاسِخ	نَسْخ		يَنْسَخُ / يَنْسَخَان / يَنْسَخُونَ	نَسَخَ / نَسَخَا / نَسَخُوا	هُوَ / هُمَا / هُمْ
				تَنْسَخُ / تَنْسَخَان / يَنْسَخْنَ	نَسَخَتْ / نَسَخَتَا / نَسَخْنَ	هِيَ / هُمَا / هُنَّ
			اِنْسَخْ / اِنْسَخَا / اِنْسَخُوا	تَنْسَخُ / تَنْسَخَان / تَنْسَخُونَ	نَسَخْتَ / سَخْتُمَا / نَسَخْتُمْ	أَنْتَ / أَنْتُمَا / أَنْتُمْ
			اِنْسَخِي / اِنْسَخَا / اِنْسَخْنَ	تَنْسَخِينَ / تَنْسَخَان / تَنْسَخْنَ	نَسَخْتِ / سَخْتُمَا / نَسَخْتُنَّ	أَنْتِ / أَنْتُمَا / أَنْتُنَّ
				أَنْسَخُ / نَنْسَخُ	نَسَخْتُ / نَسَخْنَا	أَنَا / نَحْنُ

Sentences

1. لا تَنْسَخْ الوَاجِبَات المَنْزِليَّة مِنْ أَصْدِقَائِكَ

2. هَلْ تَعْرِفُ عَنِ الكِتَاب المَنْسُوخ؟

3. هَلْ لَدَيْكَ آلَة نَسْخ لِلصُّوَرِ

English translation

1. Do not copy the homework from your friends
2. Do you know about the abrogated book?
3. Do you have a photocopier?

Verb #12 – رَتَّبَ – to organise, to order, to arrange

إِسْم الْمَفْعُول (The passive participle)	إِسْم الْفَاعِل (The active participle)	الْمَصْدَر (Verbal Noun)	أَمْرٌ (Imperative)	الْمُضَارِع (Present)	الْمَاضِي (Past)	الضَّمِير (pronoun)
مُرَتَّب	مُرَتِّب	تَرْتِيب		يُرَتِّب / يُرَتِّبَانِ / يُرَتِّبُونَ	رَتَّبَ / رَتَّبَا / رَتَّبُوا	هُوَ / هُمَا / هُمْ
				تُرَتِّب / تُرَتِّبَانِ / يُرَتِّبْنَ	رَتَّبَتْ / رَتَّبَتَا / رَتَّبْنَ	هِيَ / هُمَا / هُنَّ
			رَتِّب / رَتِّبَا / رَتِّبُوا	تُرَتِّب / تُرَتِّبَانِ / تُرَتِّبُونَ	رَتَّبْتَ / رَتَّبْتُمَا / رَتَّبْتُمْ	أَنْتَ / أَنْتُمَا / أَنْتُمْ
			رَتِّبِي / رَتِّبَا / رَتِّبْنَ	تُرَتِّبِينَ / تُرَتِّبَانِ / تُرَتِّبْنَ	رَتَّبْتِ / رَتَّبْتُمَا / رَتَّبْتُنَّ	أَنْتِ / أَنْتُمَا / أَنْتُنَّ
				أُرَتِّب / نُرَتِّب	رَتَّبْتُ / رَتَّبْنَا	أَنَا / نَحْنُ

Sentences

١. أَحْتَاجُ أَنْ أُرَتِّبَ غُرْفَتِي.

٢. رَتِّبْ حَيَاتَكَ يَا أَخِي.

٣. اِتَّبِعْ جَمِيعَ الخُطُوَات بِحَسبِ التَّرْتِيب.

English translation

1. I need to organise my room.
2. Arange your life, my brother.
3. Follow all of the steps in order.

Verb #13 – فَعَلَ – to do, to accomplish

اِسْم الْمَفْعُول (The passive participle)	اِسْم الْفَاعِل (The active participle)	الْمَصْدَر (Verbal Noun)	أَمْرٌ (Imperative)	الْمُضَارِع (Present)	الْمَاضِى (Past)	الضَّمِير (Pronoun)
مَفْعُول	فَاعِل	فَعْل		يَفْعَلُ يَفْعَلَانِ يَفْعَلُونَ	فَعَلَ فَعَلَا فَعَلُوا	هُوَ هُمَا هُمْ
				تَفْعَلُ تَفْعَلَانِ يَفْعَلْنَ	فَعَلَتْ فَعَلَتَا فَعَلْنَ	هِيَ هُمَا هُنَّ
			اِفْعَلْ اِفْعَلَا اِفْعَلُوا	تَفْعَلُ تَفْعَلَانِ تَفْعَلُونَ	فَعَلْتَ فَعَلْتُمَا فَعَلْتُمْ	أَنْتَ أَنْتُمَا أَنْتُمْ
			اِفْعَلِي اِفْعَلَا اِفْعَلْنَ	تَفْعَلِينَ تَفْعَلَانِ تَفْعَلْنَ	فَعَلْتِ فَعَلْتُمَا فَعَلْتُنَّ	أَنْتِ أَنْتُمَا أَنْتُنَّ
				أَفْعَلُ نَفْعَلُ	فَعَلْتُ فَعَلْنَا	أَنَا نَحْنُ

Sentences

١. فَعَلَ السَارِقُ الجَريمَةَ

٢. كَيْفَ سَتُخَطِّطُ لِفعْلِ كُلَّ هَذَا؟

٣. اِفْعَلْ الخَيرَات طُوْلَ حَياتِكَ

English Translation

1. The thief did the crime.
2. How will you plan to accomplish all of this?
3. Do righteous deeds throughout your life.

Verb 14- سَكَنَ – to live, to reside

اِسْم الْمَفْعُول (The passive participle)	اِسْم الْفَاعِل (The active participle)	الْمَصْدَر (Verbal Noun)	أَمْرٌ (Imperative)	الْمُضَارع (Present)	الْمَاضِى (Past)	الضَّمِير (Pronoun)
مَسْكُون	سَاكِن	سُكُون		يَسْكُنُ يَسْكُنَانِ يَسْكُنُونَ	سَكَنَ سَكَنَا سَكَنُوا	هُوَ هُمَا هُمْ
				تَسْكُنُ يَسْكُنَانِ يَسْكُنَّ	سَكَنَتْ سَكَنَا سَكَنَّ	هِيَ هُمَا هُنَّ
			أُسْكُنْ أُسْكُنَا أُسْكُنُوا	تَسْكُنُ تَسْكُنَانِ تَسْكُنُونَ	سَكَنْتَ سَكَنْتُمَا سَكَنْتُمْ	أَنْتَ أَنْتُمَا أَنْتُمْ
			أُسْكُنِي أُسْكُنَا أُسْكُنَّ	تَسْكُنِينَ تَسْكُنَانِ تَسْكُنَّ	سَكَنْتِ سَكَنْتُمَا سَكَنْتُنَّ	أَنْتِ أَنْتُمَا أَنْتُنَّ
				أَسْكُنُ نَسْكُنُ	سَكَنْتُ سَكَنَّا	أَنَا نَحْنُ

Sentences

1. أَنَا أَسْكُنُ في هَذِهِ الشّقَّةَ

2. أَرِيْدُ انْ أَسْكُنَ في بَلَدٍ مُخْتَلِفٍ في المُسْتَقْبَلِ

3. لَا تَسْكُنْ في البُيُوتِ القَدِيمَةِ

English translation

1. I live in this flat.
2. I want to live in a different country in the future.
3. Do not live in old houses.

Verb #15 – أَرَادَ – to want

اِسْم الْمَفْعُول (The passive participle)	اِسْم الْفَاعِل (The active participle)	الْمَصْدَر (Verbal Noun)	أَمْرٌ (Imperative)	الْمُضَارِع (Present)	الْمَاضِي (Past)	الضَّمِير (pronoun)
مُرَاد	مُرِيد	إِرَادَة		يُرِيدُ يُرِيدَانِ يُرِيدُونَ	أَرَادَ أَرَادَا أَرَادُوا	هُوَ هُمَا هُمْ
				تُرِيدُ تُرِيدَانِ يُرِدْنَ	أَرَادَتْ أَرَادَتَا أَرَدْنَ	هِيَ هُمَا هُنَّ
			أَرِدْ أَرِيدَا أَرِيدُوا	تُرِيدُ تُرِيدَانِ تُرِيدُونَ	أَرَدْتَ أَرَدْتُمَا أَرَدْتُمْ	أَنْتَ أَنْتُمَا أَنْتُمْ
			أَرِيدِي أَرِيدَا أَرِدْنَ	تُرِيدِينَ تُرِيدَانِ تُرِدْنَ	أَرَدْتِ أَرَدْتُمَا أَرَدْتُنَّ	أَنْتِ أَنْتُمَا أَنْتُنَّ
				أُرِيدُ نُرِيد	أَرَدْتُ أَرَدْنَا	أَنَا نَحْنُ

<u>Sentences</u>

أُرِيدُ أَنْ أَذْهَبَ اِلى الدُّكَّان.1

أَرَادَ الرَجُلُ الذَهاب اِلى بَلَدِهِ.2

لَيْسَ مِن الجَيِّدِ أَنْ تُرِيدَ كُلَّ شَيء.3

<u>English Translation</u>

1. I want to go to the shop.
2. The man wanted to go to his country.
3. It is not good to want everything.

Verb #16 – نَامَ – to sleep

اِسْم الْمَفْعُول (The passive participle)	اِسْم الْفَاعِل (The active participle)	الْمَصْدَر (Verbal Noun)	أَمْرٌ (Imperative)	الْمُضَارِع (Present)	الْمَاضِي (Past)	الضَّمِير (pronoun)
مَنُوم	نَائِم	نَوْم		يَنَامُ / يَنَامَانِ / يَنَامُونَ	نَامَ / نَامَا / نَامُوا	هُوَ / هُمَا / هُمْ
				تَنَامُ / تَنَامَانِ / يَنَمْنَ	نَامَتْ / نَامَتَا / نِمْنَ	هِيَ / هُمَا / هُنَّ
			نَمْ / نَامَا / نَامُوا	تَنَامُ / تَنَامَانِ / تَنَامُونَ	نِمْتَ / نِمْتُمَا / نِمْتُمْ	أَنْتَ / أَنْتُمَا / أَنْتُمْ
			نَامِى / نَامَا / نَمْنَ	تَنَامِينَ / تَنَامَانِ / تَنَمْنَ	نِمْتِ / نِمْتُمَا / نِمْتُنَّ	أَنْتِ / أَنْتُمَا / أَنْتُنَّ
				أَنَامُ / نَنَامُ	نِمْتُ / نِمْنَا	أَنَا / نَحْنُ

Sentences

١. نِمْتُ كَثِيراً بِالْأَمْس

٢. كَثْرَةُ النَومِ لَيْسَتْ صَحِيَّةٌ

٣. نَمْ بِاللَّيْلِ، وَ لا بِالنَّهَارِ

English Translation

1. I slept a lot yesterday.
2. Too much sleep is not healthy.
3. Sleep during the night, not during the day.

Verb #17 – اِسْتَيْقَظَ – to wake up

اِسْم الْمَفْعُول (The passive participle)	اِسْم الْفَاعِل (The active participle)	الْمَصْدَر (Verbal Noun)	أَمْرٌ (Imperative)	الْمُضَارِع (Present)	الْمَاضِي (Past)	الضَّمِير (pronoun)
مُسْتَيْقَظ	مُسْتَيْقِظ	اِسْتِيقَاظ		يَسْتَيْقِظُ يَسْتَيْقِظَانِ يَسْتَيْقِظُونَ	اِسْتَيْقَظَ اِسْتَيْقَظَا اِسْتَيْقَظُوا	هُوَ هُمَا هُمْ
				تَسْتَيْقِظُ تَسْتَيْقِظَانِ يَسْتَيْقِظْنَ	اِسْتَيْقَظَتْ اِسْتَيْقَظَتَا اِسْتَيْقَظْنَ	هِيَ هُمَا هُنَّ
			اِسْتَيْقِظْ اِسْتَيْقِظَا اِسْتَيْقِظُوا	تَسْتَيْقِظُ تَسْتَيْقِظَانِ تَسْتَيْقِظُونَ	اِسْتَيْقَظْتَ اِسْتَيْقَظْتُمَا اِسْتَيْقَظْتُمْ	أَنْتَ أَنْتُمَا أَنْتُمْ
			اِسْتَيْقِظِي اِسْتَيْقِظَا اِسْتَيْقِظْنَ	تَسْتَيْقِظِينَ تَسْتَيْقِظَانِ تَسْتَيْقِظْنَ	اِسْتَيْقَظْتِ اِسْتَيْقَظْتُمَا اِسْتَيْقَظْتُنَّ	أَنْتِ أَنْتُمَا أَنْتُنَّ
				أَسْتَيْقِظُ نَسْتَيْقِظُ	اِسْتَيْقَظْتُ اِسْتَيْقَظْنَا	أَنَا نَحْنُ

<u>Sentences</u>

‎1.لِماذَ نَحْنُ نَسْتَيْقِظُ مِنْ النَوْمِ مُتَأَخِّراً دَئِماً؟

‎2.اِسْتَيْقِظْ مُبَكِّراً يَا دَفيد

‎3.الرَجُلانِ اِسْتَيْقَظَا السَاعَة الخَامِسَة صَبَاحَاً

English Translation

1. Why do we always wake up late from sleep?
2. Wake up early, David.
3. The two men woke up at 5am.

Verb #18 – ذَهَبَ – to go, to leave

اِسْم الْمَفْعُول (The passive participle)	اِسْم الْفَاعِل (The active participle)	الْمَصْدَر (Verbal Noun)	أَمْر (Imperative)	الْمُضَارِع (Present)	الْمَاضِي (Past)	الضَّمِير (pronoun)
مَذْهُوب	ذَاهِب	ذَهَاب		يَذْهَب يَذْهَبَانِ يَذْهَبُونَ	ذَهَبَ ذَهَبَا ذَهَبُوا	هُوَ هُمَا هُمْ
				تَذْهَب تَذْهَبَانِ يَذْهَبْنَ	ذَهَبَتْ ذَهَبَتَا ذَهَبْنَ	هِيَ هُمَا هُنَّ
			اِذْهَب اِذْهَبَا اِذْهَبُوا	تَذْهَب تَذْهَبَانِ تَذْهَبُونَ	ذَهَبْتَ ذَهَبْتُمَا ذَهَبْتُمْ	أَنْتَ أَنْتُمَا أَنْتُمْ
			اِذْهَبِي اِذْهَبَا اِذْهَبْنَ	تَذْهَبِينَ تَذْهَبَانِ تَذْهَبْنَ	ذَهَبْتِ ذَهَبْتُمَا ذَهَبْتُنَّ	أَنْتِ أَنْتُمَا أَنْتُنَّ
				أَذْهَب نَذْهَب	ذَهَبْتُ ذَهَبْنَا	أَنَا نَحْنُ

Sentences

١. ذَهَبْنَ الطَّالِباتِ اِلى المُدرّسةِ.
٢. ذَهَبْتُ اِلى المُستْوصَفِ يَوْمَ السَبْتِ.
٣. سَامِحْ النَّاسَ قَبْلَ الذهابِ اِلى النَوْمِ.

English Translation

1. The students went to the teacher.
2. I went to the clinic on Saturday.
3. Forgive the people before you go to sleep.

Verb 19 – غَسَلَ – to wash, to launder, to cleanse

اِسْم الْمَفْعُول (The passive participle)	اِسْم الْفَاعِل (The active participle)	الْمَصْدَر (Verbal Noun)	أَمْرٌ (Imperative)	الْمُضَارِع (Present)	الْمَاضِي (Past)	الضَّمِير (pronoun)
مَغْسُول	غَاسِل	غَسْل		يَغْسِلُ / يَغْسِلَانِ / يَغْسِلُونَ	غَسَلَ / غَسَلَ / غَسَلُوا	هُوَ / هُمَا / هُمْ
				تَغْسِلُ / تَغْسِلَانِ / يَغْسِلْنَ	غَسَلَتْ / غَسَلَتَا / غَسَلْنَ	هِيَ / هُمَا / هُنَّ
			اِغْسِلْ / اِغْسِلَا / اِغْسِلُوا	تَغْسِلُ / تَغْسِلَانِ / تَغْسِلُونَ	غَسَلْتَ / غَسَلْتُمَا / غَسَلْتُمْ	أَنْتَ / أَنْتُمَا / أَنْتُمْ
			اِغْسِلِي / اِغْسِلَا / اِغْسِلْنَ	تَغْسِلِينَ / تَغْسِلَانِ / تَغْسِلْنَ	غَسَلْتِ / غَسَلْتُمَا / غَسَلْتُنَّ	أَنْتِ / أَنْتُمَا / أَنْتُنَّ
				أَغْسِلُ / نَغْسِلُ	غَسَلْتُ / غَسَلْنَا	أَنَا / نَحْنُ

Sentences

١. اِغْسِلْ وَجَهَكَ حِيْنَ تَسْتَيْقِظُ مِن النَّوْمِ

٢. غَسْلُ المَلابِسِ في كُلِّ اسبُوع آمْرٌ مُهِمٌّ

٣. اِغْسِلِي قَلْبَكِ مِن القَذَارَةِ

English translation

1. Wash your face when you wake up from sleep.
2. laundering your clothes every week is very important.
3. Wash your heart from the filth.

Verb #20 – كَنَسَ – to vacuum, to sweep

اِسْم الْمَفْعُول (The passive participle)	اِسْم الْفَاعِل (The active participle)	الْمَصْدَر (Verbal Noun)	أَمْرٌ (Imperative)	الْمُضَارع (Present)	الْمَاضِي (Past)	الضَّمِير (Pronoun)
مَكْنُوس	كَانِس	كِنَاسَة		يَكْنُسُ / يَكْنُسَانِ / يَكْنُسُونَ	كَنَسَ / كَنَسَا / كَنَسُوا	هُوَ / هُمَا / هُمْ
				تَكْنُسُ / تَكْنُسَانِ / يَكْنُسْنَ	كَنَسَتْ / كَنَسَتَا / كَنَسْنَ	هِيَ / هُمَا / هُنَّ
			اُكْنُسْ / اُكْنُسَا / اُكْنُسُوا	تَكْنُسُ / تَكْنُسَانِ / تَكْنُسُونَ	كَنَسْتَ / كَنَسْتُمَا / كَنَسْتُمْ	أَنْتَ / أَنْتُمَا / أَنْتُمْ
			اُكْنُسِي / اُكْنُسَا / اُكْنُسْنَ	تَكْنُسِينَ / تَكْنُسَانِ / تَكْنُسْنَ	كَنَسْتِ / كَنَسْتُمَا / كَنَسْتُنَّ	أَنْتِ / أَنْتُمَا / أَنْتُنَّ
				أَكْنُسُ / نَكْنُسُ	كَنَسْتُ / كَنَسْنَا	أَنَا / نَحْنُ

Sentences

1. كَنَسْتُ البَيْتَ لِأَنَّه كَانَ مُتَّسِخٌ
2. كَمْ مَرَّةً يَجِبُ أَنْ أَكْنُسَ مَطْبَخِي؟
3. سَاعِدْ أَهْلَكَ بِالكِنَاسَة

English translation

1. I vacummed the house because it was dirty.
2. how often should I sweep my kitchen?
3. Help your family with the sweeping.

Verb #21 – كَوَى – to iron

اِسْم الْمَفْعُول (The passive participle)	اِسْم الْفَاعِل (The active participle)	الْمَصْدَر (Verbal Noun)	أَمْرٌ (Imperative)	الْمُضَارِع (Present)	الْمَاضِي (Past)	الضَّمِير (pronoun)
مَكْوِيّ	كَاوٍ	الْكَيُّ		يَكْوِي يَكْوِيَانِ يَكْوُونَ	كَوَى كَوَيَا كَوَوْا	هُوَ هُمَا هُمْ
				تَكْوِي تَكْوِيَانِ يَكْوِينَ	كَوَتْ كَوَتَا كَوَيْنَ	هِيَ هُمَا هُنَّ
			اِكْوِ اِكْوِيَا اِكْوُوا	تَكْوِي تَكْوِيَانِ تَكْوُونَ	كَوَيْتَ كَوَيْتُمَا كَوَيْتُمْ	أَنْتَ أَنْتُمَا أَنْتُمْ
			اِكْوِي اِكْوِيَا اِكْوِينَ	تَكْوِينَ تَكْوِيَانِ تَكْوِينَ	كَوَيْتِ كَوَيْتُمَا كَوَيْتُنَّ	أَنْتِ أَنْتُمَا أَنْتُنَّ
				أَكْوِي نَكْوِي	كَوَيْتُ كَوَيْنَا	أَنَا نَحْنُ

Sentences

1.كَوَيْتُ قَمِيصِي فِي الصَبَاح

2.هَلْ يُمْكِنُكَ أَنْ تَكْوِيَ مَلَابِسِي؟

3.لا أَرْغَبُ فِي كَوَيْ الْمَلَابِس

English translations

1. I ironed my shirt in the morning.
2. Are you able to iron my clothes?
3. I don't want to iron the clothes.

Verb #22 – قَفَزَ – to jump, to leap

اِسْم الْمَفْعُول (The passive participle)	اِسْم الْفَاعِل (The active participle)	الْمَصْدَر (Verbal Noun)	أَمْرٌ (Imperative)	الْمُضَارِع (Present)	الْمَاضِي (Past)	الضَّمِير (pronoun)
مَقْفُوز	قَافِز	قَفْز		يَقْفِزُ / يَقْفِزَانِ / يَقْفِزُونَ	قَفَزَ / قَفَزَا / قَفَزُوا	هُوَ / هُمَا / هُمْ
				تَقْفِزُ / تَقْفِزَانِ / يَقْفِزْنَ	قَفَزَتْ / قَفَزَتَا / قَفَزْنَ	هِيَ / هُمَا / هُنَّ
			اِقْفِزْ / اِقْفِزَا / اِقْفِزُوا	تَقْفِزُ / تَقْفِزَانِ / تَقْفِزُونَ	قَفَزْتَ / قَفَزْتُمَا / قَفَزْتُمْ	أَنْتَ / أَنْتُمَا / أَنْتُمْ
			اِقْفِزِي / اِقْفِزَا / اِقْفِزْنَ	تَقْفِزِينَ / تَقْفِزَانِ / يَقْفِزْنَ	قَفَزْتِ / قَفَزْتُمَا / قَفَزْتُنَّ	أَنْتِ / أَنْتُمَا / أَنْتُنَّ
				أَقْفِزُ / نَقْفِزُ	قَفَزْتُ / قَفَزْنَا	أَنَا / نَحْنُ

<u>Sentences</u>

١. قَفْزَةُ الإيمَان هِيَ أَهْيَاناً كُلُّ مَا تَحْتَاجُهُ
٢. هَلْ تَسْتَمْتِعُ بِالقَفْزِة الطَويلَةِ؟
٣. قَفَزَ مُحَمَّدٌ فَوْقَ الجِدَارِ

<u>English translation</u>

1. A leap of faith is sometimes all you need.
2. Are you enjoying the long jump?
3. Muhammed jumped over the wall.

Verb #23 – أَكَلَ – to eat, to consume

اِسْم الْمَفْعُول (The passive participle)	اِسْم الْفَاعِل (The active participle)	الْمَصْدَر (Verbal Noun)	أَمْر (Imperative)	الْمُضَارِع (Present)	الْمَاضِي (Past)	الضَّمِير (pronoun)
مَأْكُول	آكِل	أَكْل		يَأْكُلُ / يَأْكُلَانِ / يَأْكُلُونَ	أَكَلَ / أَكَلَا / أَكَلُوا	هُوَ / هُمَا / هُمْ
				تَأْكُلُ / تَأْكُلَانِ / يَأْكُلْنَ	أَكَلَتْ / أَكَلَتَا / أَكَلْنَ	هِيَ / هُمَا / هُنَّ
			كُلْ / كُلَا / كُلُوا	تَأْكُلُ / تَأْكُلَانِ / تَأْكُلُونَ	أَكَلْتَ / أَكَلْتُمَا / أَكَلْتُمْ	أَنْتَ / أَنْتُمَا / أَنْتُمْ
			كُلِي / كُلَا / كُلْنَ	تَأْكُلِينَ / تَأْكُلَانِ / تَأْكُلْنَ	أَكَلْتِ / أَكَلْتُمَا / أَكَلْتُنَّ	أَنْتِ / أَنْتُمَا / أَنْتُنَّ
				آكُلُ / نَأْكُلُ	أَكَلْتُ / أَكَلْنَا	أَنَا / نَحْنُ

<u>Sentences</u>

١. مَا الطَعَامَ الذي تُحِبُّ أَنْ تَأْكُلَهُ؟
٢. لا تَأْكُلْ الطَعَامَ كُلَّها وَحْدَكَ
٣. أُحِبُّ أَكْلَ الطَعَامِ الأَفْرِيقِي التَّقْلِيدِيَّ

<u>English translation</u>

1. What food do you like to eat?
2. Don't eat the whole food alone.
3. I like to eat traditional African food.

Verb #24 – طَلَبَ – to request, to ask, to seek

اِسْم الْمَفْعُول (The passive participle)	اِسْم الْفَاعِل (The active participle)	الْمَصْدَر (Verbal Noun)	أَمْر (Imperative)	الْمُضَارِع (Present)	الْمَاضِي (Past)	الضَّمِير (Pronoun)
مَطْلُوب	طَالِب	طَلَب		يَطْلُب يَطْلَبَانِ يَطْلُبُونَ	طَلَبَ طَلَبَا طَلَبُوا	هُوَ هُمَا هُم
				تَطْلُب تَطْلَبَانِ يَطْلُبْنَ	طَلَبَتْ طَلَبَتَا طَلَبْنَ	هِيَ هُمَا هُنَّ
			أُطْلُب أُطْلُبَا أُطْلُبُوا	تَطْلُب تَطْلُبَانِ تَطْلُبُونَ	طَلَبْتَ طَلَبْتُمَا طَلَبْتُمْ	أَنْتَ أَنْتُمَا أَنْتُمْ
			أُطْلُبِي أُطْلُبَا أُطْلُبْنَ	تَطْلُبِينَ تَطْلُبَانِ تَطْلُبْنَ	طَلَبْتِ طَلَبْتُمَا طَلَبْتُنَّ	أَنْتِ أَنْتُمَا أَنْتُنَّ
				أَطْلُب نَطْلُب	طَلَبْتُ طَلَبْنَا	أَنَا نَحْنُ

Sentences

١. طَلَبَ سَعَدٌ المُسَاعَدَةَ مِن أَخِيهِ

٢. طَلَبُ العِلْمِ فَرِيضَةٌ عَلَى كُلِّ مُسْلِمٍ

٣. جَاءَ الطَّعَامُ المَطْلُوبَ مُتَأَخِّرَاً

English translation

1. Saad asked his brother for help.
2. Seeking knowledge is mandatory for every muslim.
3. The requested food arrived late.

Verb #25 – شَرِبَ – to drink

اِسْم الْمَفْعُول (The passive participle)	اِسْم الْفَاعِل (The active participle)	الْمَصْدَر (Verbal Noun)	أَمْرّ (Imperative)	الْمُضَارِع (Present)	الْمَاضِي (Past)	الضَّمِير (Pronoun)
مَشْرُوب	شَارِب	شُرْب		يَشْرَبُ / يَشْرَبَانِ / يَشْرَبُونَ	شَرِبَ / شَرِبَا / شَرِبُوا	هُوَ / هُمَا / هُمْ
				تَشْرَبُ / تَشْرَبَانِ / يَشْرَبْنَ	شَرِبَتْ / شَرِبَتَا / شَرِبْنَ	هِيَ / هُمَا / هُنَّ
			اِشْرَبْ / اِشْرَبَا / اِشْرَبُوا	تَشْرَبُ / تَشْرَبَانِ / تَشْرَبُونَ	شَرِبْتَ / شَرِبْتُمَا / شَرِبْتُمْ	أَنْتَ / أَنْتُمَا / أَنْتُمْ
			اِشْرَبِى / اِشْرَبَا / اِشْرَبْنَ	تَشْرَبِينَ / تَشْرَبَانِ / تَشْرَبْنَ	شَرِبْتِ / شَرِبْتُمَا / شَرِبْتُنَّ	أَنْتِ / أَنْتُمَا / أَنْتُنَّ
				أَشْرَبُ / نَشْرَبُ	شَرِبْتُ / شَرِبْنَا	أَنَا / نَحْنُ

Sentences

1. شَرِبَ دَيْفِيد عَصِيْرَ البُرْتُقَال

2. مَا هُوَ شَرَابَكَ الْمُفَضَّلِ؟

3. هَلْ تَشْرَبُ الشَّايَ فِي الصَبَاح؟

English translation

1. David drank orange juice.
2. What's your favourite drink?
3. Do you drink tea in the morning?

Verb #26 – حَوَّلَ – to change, to transform, to switch

اِسْم الْمَفْعُول (The passive participle)	اِسْم الْفَاعِل (The active participle)	الْمَصْدَر (Verbal Noun)	أَمْرٌ (Imperative)	الْمُضَارِع (Present)	الْمَاضِي (Past)	الضَّمِير (pronoun)
مُحَوَّل	مُحَوِّل	تَحْوِيل		يُحَوِّلُ يُحَوِّلَانِ يُحَوِّلُونَ	حَوَّلَ حَوَّلَا حَوَّلُوا	هُوَ هُمَا هُمْ
				تُحَوِّلُ تُحَوِّلَانِ يُحَوِّلْنَ	حَوَّلَتْ حَوَّلَتَا حَوَّلْنَ	هِيَ هُمَا هُنَّ
			حَوِّلْ حَوِّلَا حَوِّلُوا	تُحَوِّلُ تُحَوِّلَانِ تُحَوِّلُونَ	حَوَّلْتَ حَوَّلْتُمَا حَوَّلْتُمْ	أَنْتَ أَنْتُمَا أَنْتُمْ
			حَوِّلِي حَوِّلَا حَوِّلْنَ	تُحَوِّلِينَ تُحَوِّلَانِ تُحَوِّلْنَ	حَوَّلْتِ حَوَّلْتُمَا حَوَّلْتُنَّ	أَنْتِ أَنْتُمَا أَنْتُنَّ
				أُحَوِّلُ نُحَوِّلُ	حَوَّلْتُ حَوَّلْنَا	أَنَا نَحْنُ

<u>Sentences</u>

1. حَوِّلْ أَسْلُوْبَكَ مَعَ أُمُّكَ
2. أُرِيدُ التَحْوِيلَ مِن مَدْرَسَةٍ اِلى أُخْرَى
3. حَوِّلْ حَيَاتَكَ اِلى الأَفْضَلِ

<u>English translation</u>

1. Change your ways with your mother.
2. I want to switch from one school to another.
3. Transform your life for the better.

Verb #27- فَضَّلَ – to prefer

اِسْم الْمَفْعُول (The passive participle)	اِسْم الْفَاعِل (The active participle)	الْمَصْدَر (Verbal Noun)	أَمْرٌ (Imperative)	الْمُضَارِع (Present)	الْمَاضِي (Past)	الضَّمِير (pronoun)
مُفَضَّل	مُفَضِّل	تَفْضِيل		يُفَضِّلُ / يُفَضِّلَانِ / يُفَضِّلُونَ	فَضَّلَ / فَضَّلَا / فَضَّلُوا	هُوَ / هُمَا / هُمْ
				تُفَضِّلُ / تُفَضِّلَانِ / يُفَضِّلْنَ	فَضَّلَتْ / فَضَّلَتَا / فَضَّلْنَ	هِيَ / هُمَا / هُنَّ
			فَضِّلْ / فَضِّلَا / فَضِّلُوا	تُفَضِّلُ / تُفَضِّلَانِ / تُفَضِّلُونَ	فَضَّلْتَ / فَضَّلْتُمَا / فَضَّلْتُمْ	أَنْتَ / أَنْتُمَا / أَنْتُمْ
			فَضِّلِي / فَضِّلَا / فَضِّلْنَ	تُفَضِّلِينَ / تُفَضِّلَانِ / تُفَضِّلْنَ	فَضَّلْتِ / فَضَّلْتُمَا / فَضَّلْتُنَّ	أَنْتِ / أَنْتُمَا / أَنْتُنَّ
				أُفَضِّلُ / نُفَضِّلُ	فَضَّلْتُ / فَضَّلْنَا	أَنَا / نَحْنُ

Sentences

1.أَفَضِّلُ طَعَامَ بَلَدِي عَلَى طَعَامِ بَلَدِكَ.

2.وَللَّهُ فَضَّلَ بَعْضَكُمْ عَلَى بَعْضٍ فِي الرِّزْقِ (Quran, surah nahl, verse 71)

3.هَذَا هُوَ خِيَارِي المُفَضَّل

English translation

1. I prefer my country's food over yours.
2. And God has favoured some of you over others in sustenance.
3. That is my preferred option.

Verb #28 – عَمِلَ – to work, to do, to operate

اِسْم الْمَفْعُول (The passive participle)	اِسْم الْفَاعِل (The active participle)	الْمَصْدَر (Verbal Noun)	أَمْر (Imperative)	الْمُضَارِع (Present)	الْمَاضِي (Past)	الضَّمِير (pronoun)
مَعْمُول	عَامِل	عَمَل		يَعْمَلُ يَعْمَلَانِ يَعْمَلُونَ	عَمِلَ عَمِلَا عَمِلُوا	هُوَ هُمَا هُمْ
				تَعْمَلُ تَعْمَلَانِ يَعْمَلْنَ	عَمِلَتْ عَمِلَتَا عَمِلْنَ	هِيَ هُمَا هُنَّ
			اِعْمَلْ اِعْمَلَا اِعْمَلُوا	تَعْمَلُ تَعْمَلَانِ تَعْمَلُونَ	عَمِلْتَ عَمِلْتُمَا عَمِلْتُمْ	أَنْتَ أَنْتُمَا أَنْتُمْ
			اِعْمَلِي اِعْمَلَا اِعْمَلْنَ	تَعْمَلِينَ تَعْمَلَانِ تَعْمَلْنَ	عَمِلْتِ عَمِلْتُمَا عَمِلْتُنَّ	أَنْتِ أَنْتُمَا أَنْتُنَّ
				أَعْمَلُ نَعْمَلُ	عَمِلْتُ عَمِلْنَا	أَنَا نَحْنُ

Sentences

١.؟ أَيْنَ تَعْمَلُ في المَدِيْنَةِ؟

٢.؟ ما مَجَالُ عَمَلِكَ؟

٣. اِعْمَلُوا الوَاجِبَ المَنْزِلِي يَا إِخْوَان

English translation

1. Where do you work in the city?
2. What line of work do you work in?
3. Do the homework, brothers.

Verb #29 – سَافَرَ – to travel (comes with إلى)

اِسْم الْمَفْعُول (The passive participle)	اِسْم الْفَاعِل (The active participle)	الْمَصْدَر (Verbal Noun)	أَمْر (Imperative)	الْمُضَارِع (Present)	الْمَاضِي (Past)	الضَّمِير (Pronoun)
مُسَافَر	مُسَافِر	مُسَافَرَة		يُسَافِرُ يُسَافِرَانِ يُسَافِرُونَ	سَافَرَ سَافَرَا سَافَرُوا	هُوَ هُمَا هُمْ
				تُسَافِرُ تُسَافِرَانِ يُسَافِرْنَ	سَافَرَتْ سَافَرَتَا سَافَرْنَ	هِيَ هُمَا هُنَّ
			سَافِرْ سَافِرَا سَافِرُوا	تُسَافِرُ تُسَافِرَانِ تُسَافِرُونَ	سَافَرْتَ سَافَرْتُمَا سَافَرْتُمْ	أَنْتَ أَنْتُمَا أَنْتُمْ
			سَافِرِي سَافِرَا سَافِرْنَ	تُسَافِرِينَ تُسَافِرَانِ تُسَافِرْنَ	سَافَرْتِ سَافَرْتُمَا سَافَرْتُنَّ	أَنْتِ أَنْتُمَا أَنْتُنَّ
				أَسَافِرُ نُسَافِرُ	سَافَرْتُ سَافَرْنَا	أَنَا نَحْنُ

Sentences

1.أُرِيدُ أَنْ أَسَافِرَ اِلى الغَرْبِ في المُسْتَقبَلِ

2.أَحِبُّ المُسَافَرَةَ في الصَيْفِ

3.تَعِبَ المُسَافِرُ بَعْدَ السَفْرِ

English Translation

1. I want to travel to the west in the future.
2. I like to travel in the summer.
3. The traveller became tired after his travel.

Verb #30 اِنْتَظَرَ – to await, to expect

اِسْم الْمَفْعُول (The passive participle)	اِسْم الْفَاعِل (The active participle)	الْمَصْدَر (Verbal Noun)	أَمْرٌ (Imperative)	الْمُضَارِع (Present)	الْمَاضِي (Past)	الضَّمِير (pronoun)
مُنْتَظَر	مُنْتَظِر	اِنْتِظَار		يَنْتَظِرُ / يَنْتَظِرَانِ / يَنْتَظِرُونَ	اِنْتَظَرَ / اِنْتَظَرَا / اِنْتَظَرُوا	هُوَ / هُمَا / هُمْ
				تَنْتَظِرُ / تَنْتَظِرَانِ / يَنْتَظِرْنَ	اِنْتَظَرَتْ / اِنْتَظَرَتَا / اِنْتَظَرْنَ	هِيَ / هُمَا / هُنَّ
			اِنْتَظِرْ / اِنْتَظِرَا / اِنْتَظِرُوا	تَنْتَظِرُ / تَنْتَظِرَانِ / تَنْتَظِرُونَ	اِنْتَظَرْتَ / اِنْتَظَرْتُمَا / اِنْتَظَرْتُمْ	أَنْتَ / أَنْتُمَا / أَنْتُمْ
			اِنْتَظِرِي / اِنْتَظِرَا / اِنْتَظِرْنَ	تَنْتَظِرِينَ / تَنْتَظِرَانِ / تَنْتَظِرْنَ	اِنْتَظَرْتِ / اِنْتَظَرْتُمَا / اِنْتَظَرْتُنَّ	أَنْتِ / أَنْتُمَا / أَنْتُنَّ
				أَنْتَظِرُ / نَنْتَظِرُ	اِنْتَظَرْتُ / اِنْتَظَرْنَا	أَنَا / نَحْنُ

<u>Sentences</u>

1. اِنْتَظَرَالرَجُلُ صِدِيقَهُ عِنْدَ المَحَطَّةِ
2. اِنْتَظَرْتُ الحَافِلَةَ لِمُدَّةِ سَعاةٍ
3. إِنَّنِي أَنْتَظِرُ مِنْكَ أَخْلَاقً حَسَنَةً

English Translation

1. The man waited for his friend at the station.
2. I waited for the bus for a period of one hour.
3. I expect from you good manners.

verb #31 – اِسْتَطَاعَ – To be able to do something

اِسْم الْمَفْعُول (The passive participle)	اِسْم الْفَاعِل (The active participle	الْمَصْدَر (Verbal Noun)	أَمْرٌ (Imperative	الْمُضَارِع (Present)	الْمَاضِي (Past)	الضَّمِير (Pronoun)
مُسْتَطَاع	مُسْتَطِيع	اِسْتِطَاعَة		يَسْتَطِيعُ يَسْتَطِيعَانِ يَسْتَطِيعُونَ	اِسْتَطَاعَ اِسْتَطَاعَا اِسْتَطَاعُوا	هُوَ هُمَا هُمْ
				تَسْتَطِيعُ تَسْتَطِيعَانِ يَسْتَطِعْنَ	اِسْتَطَاعَتْ اِسْتَطَاعَتَا اِسْتَطَعْنَ	هِيَ هُمَا هُنَّ
			اِسْتَطِعْ اِسْتَطِيعَا اِسْتَطِيعُوا	تَسْتَطِيعُ تَسْتَطِيعَانِ تَسْتَطِيعُونَ	اِسْتَطَعْتَ اِسْتَطَعْتُمَا اِسْتَطَعْتُمْ	أَنْتَ أَنْتُمَا أَنْتُمْ
			اِسْتَطِيعِي اِسْتَطِيعَا اِسْتَطِعْنَ	تَسْتَطِيعِينَ تَسْتَطِيعَانِ تَسْتَطِعْنَ	اِسْتَطَعْتِ اِسْتَطَعْتُمَا اِسْتَطَعْتُنَّ	أَنْتِ أَنْتُمَا أَنْتُنَّ
				أَسْتَطِيعُ نَسْتَطِيعُ	اِسْتَطَعْتُ اِسْتَطَعْنَا	أَنَا نَحْنُ

Sentences

1.اِسْتَطَعْتُ أَنْ أَنْجَحَ فِي اِمْتِحَانَاتِي.

2.إِذَا كُنْتَ مُسْتَطِيعٌ عَلَى الصَّدَقَةٍ، فَأَنْفِقْ عَلَى الْفُقَرَاءِ.

3.اِسْتَطَاعَتْ أَنْ تَتَخَرَّج مِن الجَامِعَةِ.

English translation

1. I was able to pass my exam.
2. If you are able to give charity, then spend it on the poor.
3. She was able to graduate from university.

Verb #32 – دَرَسَ – to study

اِسْم الْمَفْعُول (The passive participle)	اِسْم الْفَاعِل (The active participle)	الْمَصْدَر (Verbal Noun)	أَمْر (Imperative)	الْمُضَارِع (Present)	الْمَاضِي (Past)	الضَّمِير (pronoun)
مَدْرُوس	دَارِس	دَرْس		يَدْرُسُ / يَدْرُسَانِ / يَدْرُسُونَ	دَرَسَ / دَرَسَا / دَرَسُوا	هُوَ / هُمَا / هُمْ
				تَدْرُسُ / تَدْرُسَانِ / يَدْرُسْنَ	دَرَسَتْ / دَرَسَتَا / دَرَسْنَ	هِيَ / هُمَا / هُنَّ
			أُدْرُسْ / أُدْرُسَا / أُدْرُسُوا	تَدْرُسُ / تَدْرُسَانِ / تَدْرُسُونَ	دَرَسْتَ / دَرَسْتُمَا / دَرَسْتُمْ	أَنْتَ / أَنْتُمَا / أَنْتُمْ
			أُدْرُسِي / أُدْرُسَا / أُدْرُسْنَ	تَدْرُسِينَ / تَدْرُسَانِ / تَدْرُسْنَ	دَرَسْتِ / دَرَسْتُمَا / دَرَسْتُنَّ	أَنْتِ / أَنْتُمَا / أَنْتُنَّ
				أَدْرُسُ / نَدْرُسُ	دَرَسْتُ / دَرَسْنَا	أَنَا / نَحْنُ

Sentences

1.دَرَسْتُ الهَنْدَسَةَ في الجَامِعَةِ.
2.أُدْرُسْ الصَّيْضَلِيَّةَ لِأَنَّ عِلْمَهُ مُفِيدٌ.
3.أُدْرُسِي لِكَيْ تَفْلِحي.

English translation

1. I studied engineering at university.
2. Study pharmacy because its knowledge is very useful.
3. Study so that you become successful.

Verb #33 – دَرَّسَ – to teach, to educate

اِسْم الْمَفْعُول (The passive participle)	اِسْم الْفَاعِل (The active participle)	الْمَصْدَر (Verbal Noun)	أَمْرٌ (Imperative)	الْمُضَارِع (Present)	الْمَاضِي (Past)	الضَّمِير (pronoun)
مُدَرَّس	مُدَرِّس	تَدْرِيس		يُدَرِّسُ يُدَرِّسَانِ يُدَرِّسُونَ	دَرَّسَ دَرَّسَا دَرَّسُوا	هُوَ هُمَا هُمْ
				تُدَرِّسُ تُدَرِّسَانِ يُدَرِّسْنَ	دَرَّسَتْ دَرَّسَتَا دَرَّسْنَ	هِيَ هُمَا هُنَّ
			دَرِّسْ دَرِّسَا دَرِّسُوا	تُدَرِّسُ تُدَرِّسَانِ تُدَرِّسُونَ	دَرَّسْتَ دَرَّسْتُمَا دَرَّسْتُمْ	أَنْتَ أَنْتُمَا أَنْتُمْ
			دَرِّسِي دَرِّسَا دَرِّسْنَ	تُدَرِّسِينَ تُدَرِّسَانِ تُدَرِّسْنَ	دَرَّسْتِ دَرَّسْتُمَا دَرَّسْتُنَّ	أَنْتِ أَنْتُمَا أَنْتُنَّ
				أُدَرِّسُ نُدَرِّسُ	دَرَّسْتُ دَرَّسْنَا	أَنَا نَحْنُ

Sentences

1.التَدْرِيسُ في الثَّانَوِيَّةُ أَفْضَلُ مِن الِابْتِدَائِيَّةِ.

2.أُرِيْدُ اَنْ أَدَرِّسَ الرِياضِات في المُسْتَقْبَل.

3.أَخِي يُدَرِّسُ في لَندَن.

English Translation

1. The teaching in high school is better than that of the primary school.
2. I want to teach maths in the future.
3. My brother is teaching in London.

Verb #34 – بَدَأَ – to start, to begin, to commence

اِسْم الْمَفْعُول (The passive participle)	اِسْم الْفَاعِل (The active participle)	الْمَصْدَر (Verbal Noun)	أَمْرّ (Imperative)	الْمُضَارِع (Present)	الْمَاضِي (Past)	الضَّمِير (pronoun)
مَبْدُوء	بَادِئ	بَدْء		يَبْدَأُ / يَبْدَآنِ / يَبْدَأُونَ	بَدَأَ / بَدَآ / بَدَأُوا	هُوَ / هُمَا / هُمْ
				تَبْدَأُ / تَبْدَآنِ / يَبْدَأْنَ	بَدَأَتْ / بَدَأَتَا / بَدَأْنَ	هِيَ / هُمَا / هُنَّ
			اِبْدَأْ / اِبْدَآ / اِبْدَأُوا	تَبْدَأُ / تَبْدَآنِ / تَبْدَأُونَ	بَدَأْتَ / بَدَأْتُمَا / بَدَأْتُمْ	أَنْتَ / أَنْتُمَا / أَنْتُمْ
			اِبْدَئِي / اِبْدَآ / اِبْدَأْنَ	تَبْدَئِينَ / تَبْدَآنِ / تَبْدَأْنَ	بَدَأْتِ / بَدَأْتُمَا / بَدَأْتُنَّ	أَنْتِ / أَنْتُمَا / أَنْتُنَّ
				أَبْدَأُ / نَبْدَأُ	بَدَأْتُ / بَدَأْنَا	أَنَا / نَحْنُ

<u>Sentences</u>

١. بَدَأْتُ دِرَاسَةَ اللُغَةَ العَرَبِيَّةَ
٢. اِبْدَأْ يَوْمَكَ بِتَغْسِيلِ وَجْهِكَ
٣. بَدَأَتْ فَاطِمَةُ رِحْلَتَهَا فِي البَحْثِ عَن العِلْمِ

<u>English translation</u>

1. I started learning arabic.
2. Start your day by washing your face.
3. Fatima began her journey in seeking knowledge.

Verb #35 اِنْتَهَى – to end, to finish

اِسْم الْمَفْعُول (The passive participle)	اِسْم الْفَاعِل (The active participle)	الْمَصْدَر (Verbal Noun)	أَمْرٌ (Imperative)	الْمُضَارِع (Present)	الْمَاضِى (Past)	الضَّمِير (Pronoun)
مُنْتَهًى	مُنْتَهٍ	اِنْتِهَاء		يَنْتَهِي يَنْتَهِيَانِ يَنْتَهُونَ	اِنْتَهَى اِنْتَهَيَا اِنْتَهَوْا	هُوَ هُمَا هُم
				تَنْتَهِي تَنْتَهِيَانِ يَنْتَهِينَ	اِنْتَهَت اِنْتَهَتَا اِنْتَهَيْنَ	هِيَ هُمَا هُنَّ
			اِنْتَهِ اِنْتَهِيَا اِنْتَهُوا	تَنْتَهِي تَنْتَهِيَانِ تَنْتَهُونَ	اِنْتَهَيْت اِنْتَهَيْتُمَا اِنْتَهَيْتُم	أَنْتَ أَنْتُمَا أَنْتُم
			اِنْتَهِي اِنْتَهِيَا اِنْتَهِينَ	تَنْتَهِينَ تَنْتَهِيَانِ تَنْتَهِينَ	اِنْتَهَيْتِ اِنْتَهَيْتُمَا اِنْتَهَيْتُنَّ	أَنْتِ أَنْتُمَا أَنْتُنَّ
				أَنْتَهِي نَنْتَهِي	اِنْتَهَيْت اِنْتَهَيْنَا	أَنَا نَحْنُ

Sentences

1. أَخِيراً اِنْتَهَيْتُ وَاجِبَاتي الْمَنْزِلِيَّةِ.
2. أُريدُ اِنْتِهَاء هَذهِ العَلَاقةِ.
3. لا أَسْتَطِيعُ الإنْتِظَارَ لِاِنْتِهَاء هَذهِ السَنَةَ.

English translation

1. I finally finished my homework.
2. I want this relationship to end.
3. I cannot wait for this year to end.

Verb #36 – رَسَمَ – to draw, to paint

اِسْم الْمَفْعُول (The passive participle)	اِسْم الْفَاعِل (The active participle)	الْمَصْدَر (Verbal Noun)	أَمْر (Imperative)	الْمُضَارِع (Present)	الْمَاضِي (Past)	الضَّمِير (pronoun)
مَرْسُوم	رَاسِم	رَسْم		يَرْسُمُ / يَرْسُمَانِ / يَرْسُمُونَ	رَسَمَ / رَسَمَا / رَسَمُوا	هُوَ / هُمَا / هُمْ
				تَرْسُمُ / تَرْسُمَانِ / يَرْسُمْنَ	رَسَمَتْ / رَسَمَتَا / رَسَمْنَ	هِيَ / هُمَا / هُنَّ
			أُرْسُمْ / أُرْسُمَا / أُرْسُمُوا	تَرْسُمُ / تَرْسُمَانِ / تَرْسُمُونَ	رَسَمْتَ / رَسَمْتُمَا / رَسَمْتُمْ	أَنْتَ / أَنْتُمَا / أَنْتُمْ
			أُرْسُمِي / أُرْسُمَا / أُرْسُمْنَ	تَرْسُمِينَ / تَرْسُمَانِ / تَرْسُمْنَ	رَسَمْتِ / رَسَمْتُمَا / رَسَمْتُنَّ	أَنْتِ / أَنْتُمَا / أَنْتُنَّ
				أَرْسُمُ / نَرْسُمُ	رَسَمْتُ / رَسَمْنَا	أَنَا / نَحْنُ

Sentences

1.أُحِبُّ انْ أَرْسُمَ في وَقْتِ الفَرَاغ
2.الرَسْمُ مِن أَفْضَل الانْشِطَة التَّرْفِيهِيِّ
3.هَلْ تُحِبُّ رَسْمَ الوُجُوهِ أَو الحَيْوَانَات؟

English translation

1. I like to draw in my free time.
2. Drawing is from the best leisure activities.
3. Do you like painting faces or animals?

Verb #37 – أَصْبَحَ – to become, to wake up, to turn into

اِسْم الْمَفْعُول (The passive participle)	اِسْم الْفَاعِل (The active participle)	الْمَصْدَر (Verbal Noun)	أَمْر (Imperative)	الْمُضَارِع (Present)	الْمَاضِي (Past)	الضَّمِير (Pronoun)
مُصْبَح	مُصْبِح	إصْبَاح		يُصْبِح يُصْبِحَانِ يُصْبِحُونَ	أَصْبَحَ أَصْبَحَا أَصْبَحُوا	هُوَ هُمَا هُمْ
				تُصْبِح تُصْبِحَانِ يُصْبِحْنَ	أَصْبَحَتْ أَصْبَحَتَا أَصْبَحْنَ	هِيَ هُمَا هُنَّ
			أَصْبِح أَصْبِحَا أَصْبِحُوا	تُصْبِح تُصْبِحَانِ تُصْبِحُونَ	أَصْبَحْتَ أَصْبَحْتُمَا أَصْبَحْتُمْ	أَنْتَ أَنْتُمَا أَنْتُمْ
			أَصْبِحِي أَصْبِحَا أَصْبِحْنَ	تُصْبِحِينَ تُصْبِحَانِ تُصْبِحْنَ	أَصْبَحْتِ أَصْبَحْتُمَا أَصْبَحْتُنَّ	أَنْتِ أَنْتُمَا أَنْتُنَّ
				أُصْبِح نُصْبِح	أَصْبَحْتُ أَصْبَحْنَا	أَنَا نَحْنُ

Sentences

1.أُرِيدُ اَنْ أُصْبِحَ رَجُلَ غَنِيًّ

2.أَصْبَحْتُ مِن النَّوْمِ غَاضِبٌ

3.أَنْتَ تُصْبِحُ مِثْلَ هَذَا الْوَحْشِ!

English translation

1. I want to become a rich man.
2. I woke up angry from sleep.
3. You are becoming such a monster!

Verb #38 – مَلَأَ – to fill

اِسْم الْمَفْعُول (The passive participle)	اِسْم الْفَاعِل (The active participle)	الْمَصْدَر (Verbal Noun)	أَمْرٌ (Imperative)	الْمُضَارِع (Present)	الْمَاضِي (Past)	الضَّمِير (pronoun)
مَمْلُوء	مَالِئ	مَلْءٌ		يَمْلَأُ / يَمْلَآنِ / يَمْلَأُونَ	مَلَأَ / مَلَآ / مَلَأُوا	هُوَ / هُمَا / هُمْ
				تَمْلَأُ / تَمْلَآنِ / يَمْلَأْنَ	مَلَأَتْ / مَلَآتَا / مَلَأْنَ	هِيَ / هُمَا / هُنَّ
			اِمْلَأْ / اِمْلَآ / اِمْلَأُوا	تَمْلَأُ / تَمْلَآنِ / تَمْلَأُونَ	مَلَأْتَ / مَلَأْتُمَا / مَلَأْتُمْ	أَنْتَ / أَنْتُمَا / أَنْتُمْ
			اِمْلَئِي / اِمْلَآ / اِمْلَأْنَ	تَمْلَئِينَ / تَمْلَآنِ / تَمْلَأْنَ	مَلَأْتِ / مَلَأْتُمَا / مَلَأْتُنَّ	أَنْتِ / أَنْتُمَا / أَنْتُنَّ
				أَمْلَأُ / نَمْلَأُ	مَلَأْتُ / مَلَأْنَا	أَنَا / نَحْنُ

<u>Sentences</u>

1.مَلَأْتُ الكُوْبَ بِالمَاءِ

2.لا تَمْلَأْ كَأْسَكَ بِالْكَافِين

3.اِمْلَأْ قَلْبَكَ بِذِكْرِ اللهِ

<u>English Translation</u>

1. I filled the cup with water.
2. Do not fill up your cup with caffeine.
3. Fill your heart with the remembrance of God.

Verb #39 – اِخْتَارَ – to choose/to select

اِسْم الْمَفْعُول (The passive participle)	اِسْم الْفَاعِل (The active participle)	الْمَصْدَر (Verbal Noun)	أَمْرٌ (Imperative)	الْمُضَارِع (Present)	الْمَاضِي (Past)	الضَّمِير (Pronoun)
مُخْتَار	مُخْتَار	اِخْتِيار		يَخْتَارُ / يَخْتَارَانِ / يَخْتَارُونَ	اِخْتَارَ / اِخْتَارَا / اِخْتَارُوا	هُوَ / هُمَا / هُمْ
				تَخْتَارُ / تَخْتَارَانِ / يَخْتَرْنَ	اِخْتَارَتْ / اِخْتَارَتَا / اِخْتَرْنَ	هِيَ / هُمَا / هُنَّ
			اِخْتَرْ / اِخْتَارَا / اِخْتَارُوا	تَخْتَارُ / تَخْتَارَانِ / تَخْتَارُونَ	اِخْتَرْتَ / اِخْتَرْتُمَا / اِخْتَرْتُمْ	أَنْتَ / أَنْتُمَا / أَنْتُمْ
			اِخْتَارِي / اِخْتَارَا / اِخْتَرْنَ	تَخْتَارِينَ / تَخْتَارَانِ / تَخْتَرْنَ	اِخْتَرْتِ / اِخْتَرْتُمَا / اِخْتَرْتُنَّ	أَنْتِ / أَنْتُمَا / أَنْتُنَّ
				أَخْتَارُ / نَخْتَارُ	اِخْتَرْتُ / اِخْتَرْنَا	أَنَا / نَحْنُ

<u>Sentences</u>

1. اِخْتَارَ رَمُحَمَّدُ اَنْ يَدْرُسَ فِي الشَرْقِ

2. اِخْتَرْ أَصْدِقَئَكَ بِعِنَايَةٍ

3. لَدَيْكَ العَدِيدُ مِن الخِيَارَاتِ فِي الحَيَاةِ

<u>English translation</u>

1. Muhammad chose to study in the east.
2. Choose your friends carefully.
3. You have so many choices in life.

Verb #40 – سَاقَ – to drive

اِسْم الْمَفْعُول (The passive participle)	اِسْم الْفَاعِل (The active participle)	الْمَصْدَر (Verbal Noun)	أَمْر (Imperative)	الْمُضَارِع (Present)	الْمَاضِي (Past)	الضَّمِير (pronoun)
مَسُوق	سَائِق	سَوْق		يَسُوقُ / يَسُوقَانِ / يَسُوقُونَ	سَاقَ / سَاقَا / سَاقُوا	هُوَ / هُمَا / هُمْ
				تَسُوقُ / تَسُوقَانِ / يَسُقْنَ	سَاقَتْ / سَاقَتَا / سُقْنَ	هِيَ / هُمَا / هُنَّ
			سُقْ / سُوقَا / سُوقُوا	تَسُوقُ / تَسُوقَانِ / تَسُوقُونَ	سُقْتَ / سُقْتُمَا / سُقْتُمْ	أَنْتَ / أَنْتُمَا / أَنْتُمْ
			سُوقِي / سُوقَا / سُقْنَ	تَسُوقِينَ / تَسُوقَانِ / تَسُقْنَ	سُقْتِ / سُقْتُمَا / سُقْتُنَّ	أَنْتِ / أَنْتُمَا / أَنْتُنَّ
				أَسُوقُ / نَسُوقُ	سُقْتُ / سُقْنَا	أَنَا / نَحْنُ

Sentences

1.أَحِبُّ أَنْ أَسُوقَ السَّيَارَاتِ الْأَلْمَانِيَّة

2.بَدَأْتُ أَنْ أَسُوقَ عِنْدَمَا كُنْتُ في الثَامِنَةِ عَشْرَةَ مِنْ عُمْرِي

3.لا تَسُوْقْ بِهَذِه السُرْعَةِ مَرَّةً أُخْرَى

English translation

1. I like to drive german cars.
2. I started driving when I was eighteen years old.
3. Do not drive that fast again!

Verb #41 – أَتَى – to come, to arrive, to show up

اِسْم الْمَفْعُول (The passive participle)	اِسْم الْفَاعِل (The active participle)	الْمَصْدَر (Verbal Noun)	أَمْرٌ (Imperative)	الْمُضَارع (Present)	الْمَاضِي (Past)	الضَّمِير (pronoun)
مَأْتِيّ	آتٍ	إِتْيَان		يَأْتِي يَأْتِيَانِ يَأْتُونَ	أَتَى أَتَيَا أَتَوْا	هُوَ هُمَا هُمْ
				تَأْتِي تَأْتِيَانِ يَأْتِينَ	أَتَتْ أَتَتَا أَتَيْنَ	هِيَ هُمَا هُنَّ
			اِيتِ اِيتِيَا اِيتُوا	تَأْتِي تَأْتِيَانِ تَأْتُونَ	أَتَيْتَ أَتَيْتُمَا أَتَيْتُمْ	أَنْتَ أَنْتُمَا أَنْتُمْ
			اِيتِي اِيتِيَا اِيتِينَ	تَأْتِينَ تَأْتِيَانِ تَأْتِينَ	أَتَيْتِ أَتَيْتُمَا أَتَيْتُنَّ	أَنْتِ أَنْتُمَا أَنْتُنَّ
				آتِي نَأْتِي	أَتَيْتُ أَتَيْنَا	أَنَا نَحْنُ

Sentences

1. أَتَيْتُ اِلى المَهرِجَان في العُطْلَةِ الأُسْبُوعِيَّةِ
2. أَتَتْ اِلى العَميدِ في الْمَسَاءِ
3. أَنَا لَمْ آتِي بِوَاسِطَةِ الحَافِلَةِ

English translation

1. I came to the festival on the weekend.
2. She came to the dean in the evening.
3. I did not arrive by bus.

Verb #42 – دَعَا – to invite, to call upon

اِسْم الْمَفْعُول (The passive participle)	اِسْم الْفَاعِل (The active participle)	الْمَصْدَر (Verbal Noun)	أَمْرٌ (Imperative)	الْمُضَارِع (Present)	الْمَاضِي (Past)	الضَّمِير (pronoun)
مَدْعُوّ	دَاع	دُعَاء		يَدْعُو / يَدْعُوَانِ / يَدْعُونَ	دَعَا / دَعَوَا / دَعَوْا	هُوَ / هُمَا / هُمْ
				تَدْعُو / تَدْعُوَانِ / يَدْعُونَ	دَعَتْ / دَعَتَا / دَعَوْنَ	هِيَ / هُمَا / هُنَّ
			أُدْعُ / أُدْعُوَا / أُدْعُوا	تَدْعُو / تَدْعُوَانِ / تَدْعُونَ	دَعَوْتَ / دَعَوْتُمَا / دَعَوْتُمْ	أَنْتَ / أَنْتُمَا / أَنْتُمْ
			أُدْعِي / أُدْعُوَا / أُدْعُونَ	تَدْعِينَ / تَدْعُوَانِ / تَدْعُونَ	دَعَوْتِ / دَعَوْتُمَا / دَعَوْتُنَّ	أَنْتِ / أَنْتُمَا / أَنْتُنَّ
				أَدْعُو / نَدْعُو	دَعَوْتُ / دَعَوْنَا	أَنَا / نَحْنُ

<u>Sentences</u>

1. دَعَوْتُ اللهَ فِي الشِّدَّةِ وَ الرَخَاءِ

2. دَعَوْنَا عَمَّنَا اِلى المَنْزِلِ لِلفَطُوْرِ

3. لِمَاذَ أَنْتُمْ تَدْعُونَ اِلى الشَّرِّ؟

<u>English translation</u>

1. I called upon God in a time of hardship and prosperity.
2. We invited our uncle to our house for breakfast.
3. Why are you guys calling to evil?

Verb #43 – تَرَكَ – to leave, to quit

اِسْم الْمَفْعُول (The passive participle)	اِسْم الْفَاعِل (The active participle)	الْمَصْدَر (Verbal Noun)	أَمْرٌ (Imperative)	الْمُضَارِع (Present)	الْمَاضِي (Past)	الضَّمِير (pronoun)
مَتْرُوك	تَارِك	تَرْك		يَتْرُكُ / يَتْرُكَانِ / يَتْرُكُونَ	تَرَكَ / تَرَكَا / تَرَكُوا	هُوَ / هُمَا / هُمْ
				تَتْرُكُ / تَتْرُكَانِ / يَتْرُكْنَ	تَرَكَتْ / تَرَكَتَا / تَرَكْنَ	هِيَ / هُمَا / هُنَّ
			اُتْرُكْ / اُتْرُكَا / اُتْرُكُوا	تَتْرُكُ / تَتْرُكَانِ / تَتْرُكُونَ	تَرَكْتَ / تَرَكْتُمَا / تَرَكْتُمْ	أَنْتَ / أَنْتُمَا / أَنْتُمْ
			اُتْرُكِي / اُتْرُكَا / اُتْرُكْنَ	تَتْرُكِينَ / تَتْرُكَانِ / تَتْرُكْنَ	تَرَكْتِ / تَرَكْتُمَا / تَرَكْتُنَّ	أَنْتِ / أَنْتُمَا / أَنْتُنَّ
				أَتْرُكُ / نَتْرُكُ	تَرَكْتُ / تَرَكْنَا	أَنَا / نَحْنُ

Sentences

1. اِضْطَرَرْتُ اِلى تَرْكِ كُرَةُ القَدَمِ بِسَبَب إصَابَةٍ

2. أُتْرُكُ مَا لا يَنْفَعَكَ

3. لِمَاذَ تَرَكْتُنَّ الذَهَابَ اِلى الصَّفِ؟

English translation

1. I had to leave football because of an injury.
2. leave out what is not benefiting you.
3. Why did you quit coming to class?

Verb #44 – بَقِيَ – to stay, remain, rest of

اِسْم الْمَفْعُول (The passive participle)	اِسْم الْفَاعِل (The active participle)	الْمَصْدَر (Verbal Noun)	أَمْر (Imperative)	الْمُضَارِع (Present)	الْمَاضِي (Past)	الضَّمِير (pronoun)
مَبْقِيّ	بَاقٍ	بَقَاء		يَبْقَى يَبْقَيَانِ يَبْقَوْنَ	بَقِيَ بَقِيَا بَقُوا	هُوَ هُمَا هُمْ
				تَبْقَى تَبْقَيَانِ يَبْقَيْنَ	بَقِيَتْ بَقِيَتَا بَقِينَ	هِيَ هُمَا هُنَّ
			اِبْقَ اِبْقَيَا اِبْقَوْا	تَبْقَى تَبْقَيَانِ تَبْقَوْنَ	بَقِيتَ بَقِيتُمَا بَقِيتُمْ	أَنْتَ أَنْتُمَا أَنْتُمْ
			اِبْقَى اِبْقَيَا اِبْقَيْنَ	تَبْقَيْنَ تَبْقَيَانِ تَبْقَيْنَ	بَقِيتِ بَقِيتُمَا بَقِيتُنَّ	أَنْتِ أَنْتُمَا أَنْتُنَّ
				أَبْقَى نَبْقَى	بَقِيتُ بَقِينَا	أَنَا نَحْنُ

<u>Sentences</u>

١. بَقِيَ قَلِيلٌ مِن الوَقْتِ

٢. حَضَرَ الفَصْلَ شَخْصٌ وَاحِدٌ، و غَابَ بَقِيَّةُ الفَصْلِ

٣. خُذْ مَا بَقِيَ مِن المَالِ

<u>English translation</u>

1. A little amount of time is left.
2. One person attended the class, and the rest of the class were absent.
3. Take the remaining of the money.

Verb #45 – لَعِبَ – to play

اِسْم الْمَفْعُول (The passive participle)	اِسْم الْفَاعِل (The active participle)	الْمَصْدَر (Verbal Noun)	أَمْر (Imperative)	الْمُضَارِع (Present)	الْمَاضِي (Past)	الضَّمِير (pronoun)
مَلْعُوب	لَاعِب	لَعْب		يَلْعَبُ / يَلْعَبَانِ / يَلْعَبُونَ	لَعِبَ / لَعِبَا / لَعِبُوا	هُوَ / هُمَا / هُمْ
				تَلْعَبُ / تَلْعَبَانِ / يَلْعَبْنَ	لَعِبَتْ / لَعِبَتَا / لَعِبْنَ	هِيَ / هُمَا / هُنَّ
			اِلْعَبْ / اِلْعَبَا / اِلْعَبُوا	تَلْعَبُ / تَلْعَبَانِ / تَلْعَبُونَ	لَعِبْتَ / لَعِبْتُمَا / لَعِبْتُمْ	أَنْتَ / أَنْتُمَا / أَنْتُمْ
			اِلْعَبِي / اِلْعَبَا / اِلْعَبْنَ	تَلْعَبِينَ / تَلْعَبَانِ / تَلْعَبْنَ	لَعِبْتِ / لَعِبْتُمَا / لَعِبْتُنَّ	أَنْتِ / أَنْتُمَا / أَنْتُنَّ
				أَلْعَبُ / نَلْعَبُ	لَعِبْتُ / لَعِبْنَا	أَنَا / نَحْنُ

<u>Sentences</u>

1. اِلْعَبْ مَعَ أَوْلَادِكَ دَائِمًا.
2. كَثْرَةُ اللَعِبِ لَيْسَ جَيِّدً.
3. لا تَلْعَبْ بِدِرَاسَتِكَ.

<u>English translation</u>

1. Play with your kids often.
2. Too much playing is not good.
3. Don't play with your studies.

Verb #46 – نَادَى – to call, to shout

اِسْم الْمَفْعُول (The passive participle)	اِسْم الْفَاعِل (The active participle)	الْمَصْدَر (Verbal Noun)	أَمْر (Imperative)	الْمُضَارِع (Present)	الْمَاضِي (Past)	الضّمِير (pronoun)
مُنَادَى	مُنَادٍ	مُنَادَاة		يُنَادِي / يُنَادِيَانِ / يُنَادُونَ	نَادَى / نَادَيَا / نَادَوْا	هُوَ / هُمَا / هُمْ
				تُنَادِي / تُنَادِيَانِ / يُنَادِينَ	نَادَتْ / نَادَتَا / نَادَيْنَ	هِيَ / هُمَا / هُنَّ
			نَادِ / نَادِيَا / نَادُوا	تُنَادِي / تُنَادِيَانِ / تُنَادُونَ	نَادَيْتَ / نَادَيْتُمَا / نَادَيْتُمْ	أَنْتَ / أَنْتُمَا / أَنْتُمْ
			نَادِي / نَادِيَا / نَادِينَ	تُنَادِينَ / تُنَادِيَانِ / تُنَادِينَ	نَادَيْتِ / نَادَيْتُمَا / نَادَيْتُنَّ	أَنْتِ / أَنْتُمَا / أَنْتُنَّ
				أُنَادِي / نُنَادِي	نَادَيْتُ / نَادَيْنَا	أَنَا / نَحْنُ

Sentences

1. نَادَى الرَجُلُ أَخِيهِ فِي الْمَحَطَّةِ و لَكِنْ لَمْ يَسْمَعْهُ.
2. إذَا أَحْتَجْتَ لِشَيْءٍ، نَادِنِي.
3. نَادِينِي عِنْدَماَ تَذْهَبُ اِلى الْمَدْرَسَةِ.

English translation

1. The man called his brother at the station but he didn't hear him.
2. If you need anything, call me.
3. Call me when you go to school.

Verb #47 – نَتَجَ – as a result of, to produce – when it comes with عَنْ it means as a result of.

اِسْم الْمَفْعُول (The passive participle)	اِسْم الْفَاعِل (The active participle)	الْمَصْدَر (Verbal Noun)	أَمْرٌ (Imperative)	الْمُضَارِع (Present)	الْمَاضِي (Past)	الضَّمِير (pronoun)
مَنْتُوج	نَاتِج	إِنْتَاج		يَنْتِجُ / يَنْتِجَانِ / يَنْتِجُونَ	نَتَجَ / نَتَجَا / نَتَجُوا	هُوَ / هُمَا / هُمْ
				تَنْتِجُ / تَنْتِجَانِ / يَنْتِجْنَ	نَتَجَتْ / نَتَجَتَا / نَتَجْنَ	هِيَ / هُمَا / هُنَّ
			اِنْتِجْ / اِنْتِجَا / اِنْتِجُوا	تَنْتِجُ / تَنْتِجَانِ / تَنْتِجُونَ	نَتَجْتَ / نَتَجْتُمَا / نَتَجْتُمْ	أَنْتَ / أَنْتُمَا / أَنْتُمْ
			اِنْتِجِي / اِنْتِجَا / اِنْتِجْنَ	تَنْتِجِينَ / تَنْتِجَانِ / تَنْتِجْنَ	نَتَجْتِ / نَتَجْتُمَا / نَتَجْتُنَّ	أَنْتِ / أَنْتُمَا / أَنْتُنَّ
				أَنْتِجُ / نَنْتِجُ	نَتَجْتُ / نَتَجْنَا	أَنَا / نَحْنُ

Sentences

1.نَتَجَ عَنْ أَفْعَالِكَ، طُرِدْتَ مِن الجَامِعَةِ

2.لَمْ تُنْتَجْ هَذهِ السِلْعَةَ في هَذا البَلَدِ

3.نُسَافِرُ الى الصِين لِإنْتَاج مَلابِسَنَا

English translation

1. As a result of your actions, you have been expelled from the university.
2. This product was not produced in this country.
3. We travel to china to produce our clothes.

Verb #48 – قَابَلَ – to meet, to interview, to encounter

اِسْم الْمَفْعُول (The passive participle)	اِسْم الْفَاعِل (The active participle)	الْمَصْدَر (Verbal Noun)	أَمْرٌ (Imperative)	الْمُضَارِع (Present)	الْمَاضِي (Past)	الضَّمِير (pronoun)
مُقَابَل	مُقَابِل	مُقَابَلَة		يُقَابِلُ يُقَابِلَانِ يُقَابِلُونَ	قَابَلَ قَابَلَا قَابَلُوا	هُوَ هُمَا هُمْ
				تُقَابِلُ تُقَابِلَانِ يُقَابِلْنَ	قَابَلَتْ قَابَلَتَا قَابَلْنَ	هِيَ هُمَا هُنَّ
			قَابِلْ قَابِلَا قَابِلُوا	تُقَابِلُ تُقَابِلَانِ تُقَابِلُونَ	قَابَلْتَ قَابَلْتُمَا قَابَلْتُمْ	أَنْتَ أَنْتُمَا أَنْتُمْ
			قَابِلِي قَابِلَا قَابِلْنَ	تُقَابِلِينَ تُقَابِلَانِ تُقَابِلْنَ	قَابَلْتِ قَابَلْتُمَا قَابَلْتُنَّ	أَنْتِ أَنْتُمَا أَنْتُنَّ
				أُقَابِلُ نُقَابِلُ	قَابَلْتُ قَابَلْنَا	أَنَا نَحْنُ

Sentences

1.لَدَيْنَا مُقَابَلَةٌ بَيْنَ وَالِدِي و المُدِيرِ

2.قَابَلْتُ زَوْجَتِي فِي الجَامِعَةِ

3.قَابَلْتُ مَالِكُ العَقَارِ القَدِيمِ فِي المَتْجَرِ

English translation

1. We have an interview between my father and the head teacher.
2. I met my wife at university.
3. I encountered my old landlord in the store.

Verb #49 – كَتَبَ – to write, to prescribe, to record

اِسْم الْمَفْعُول (The passive participle)	اِسْم الْفَاعِل (The active participle)	الْمَصْدَر (Verbal Noun)	أَمْرٌ (Imperative)	الْمُضَارِع (Present)	الْمَاضِي (Past)	الضَّمِير (Pronoun)
مَكْتُوب	كَاتِب	كِتَابَة		يَكْتُبُ يَكْتُبَانِ يَكْتُبُونَ	كَتَبَ كَتَبَا كَتَبُوا	هُوَ هُمَا هُمْ
				تَكْتُبُ تَكْتُبَانِ يَكْتُبْنَ	كَتَبَتْ كَتَبَتَا كَتَبْنَ	هِيَ هُمَا هُنَّ
			أُكْتُبْ أُكْتُبَا أُكْتُبُوا	تَكْتُبُ تَكْتُبَانِ تَكْتُبُونَ	كَتَبْتَ كَتَبْتُمَا كَتَبْتُمْ	أَنْتَ أَنْتُمَا أَنْتُمْ
			أُكْتُبِي أُكْتُبَا أُكْتُبْنَ	تَكْتُبِينَ تَكْتُبَانِ تَكْتُبْنَ	كَتَبْتِ كَتَبْتُمَا كَتَبْتُنَّ	أَنْتِ أَنْتُمَا أَنْتُنَّ
				أَكْتُبُ نَكْتُبُ	كَتَبْتُ كَتَبْنَا	أَنَا نَحْنُ

Sentences

١.أَحِبُّ كِتَابَةَ الْمُلَاحَظَات أَثْنَاء الْفَصْلِ الدِرَاسِي
٢.كَتَبَ الْمُدَرِّسُ اِسْمِي عَلَى اللَوْحَةِ
٣.أَكْرَهُ كِتَابَةً يَدِي

English Translation

1. I like to take notes during class.
2. The teacher wrote my name on the notice board.
3. I hate my hand writing.

Verb #50 – وَجَدَ – to find

اِسْم الْمَفْعُول (The passive participle)	اِسْم الْفَاعِل (The active participle)	الْمَصْدَر (Verbal Noun)	أَمْر (Imperative)	الْمُضَارِع (Present)	الْمَاضِي (Past)	الضَّمِير (pronoun)
مَوْجُود	وَاجِد	وُجُود		يَجِدُ / يَجِدَانِ / يَجِدُونَ	وَجَدَ / وَجَدَا / وَجَدُوا	هُوَ / هُمَا / هُمْ
				تَجِدُ / تَجِدَانِ / يَجِدْنَ	وَجَدَتْ / وَجَدَتَا / وَجَدْنَ	هِيَ / هُمَا / هُنَّ
			جِدْ / جِدَا / جِدُوا	تَجِدُ / تَجِدَانِ / تَجِدُونَ	وَجَدْتَ / وَجَدْتُمَا / وَجَدْتُمْ	أَنْتَ / أَنْتُمَا / أَنْتُمْ
			جِدِي / جِدَا / جِدْنَ	تَجِدِينَ / تَجِدَانِ / تَجِدْنَ	وَجَدْتِ / وَجَدْتُمَا / وَجَدْتُنَّ	أَنْتِ / أَنْتُمَا / أَنْتُنَّ
				أَجِدُ / نَجِدُ	وَجَدْتُ / وَجَدْنَا	أَنَا / نَحْنُ

Sentences

١.وَجَدَتْ الِامْرَاةُ حَقِيْبَتَهَا
٢.وُجِدَ الفَتَى المَفْقُود
٣.اِسْعَىْ فِي عَمَلِكَ، سَتَجِدُ النَجَاح

English translation

1. The women found her bag.
2. The missing boy was found.
3. Strive in your work, and you will find success.

Verb #51 – أَكَّدَ – to confirm, to affirm

اِسْم الْمَفْعُول (The passive participle)	اِسْم الْفَاعِل (The active participle)	الْمَصْدَر (Verbal Noun)	أَمْرٌ (Imperative)	الْمُضَارِع (Present)	الْمَاضِى (Past)	الضَّمِير (Pronoun)
مُؤَكَّد	مُؤَكِّد	تَأْكِيد		يُؤَكِّدُ / يُؤَكِّدَان / يُؤَكِّدُونَ	أَكَّدَ / أَكَّدَا / أَكَّدُوا	هُوَ / هُمَا / هُمْ
				تُؤَكِّدُ / تُؤَكِّدَانِ / يُؤَكِّدْنَ	أَكَّدَتْ / أَكَّدَا / أَكَّدْنَ	هِيَ / هُمَا / هُنَّ
			أَكِّدْ / أَكِّدَا / أَكِّدُوا	تُؤَكِّدُ / تُؤَكِّدَانِ / تُؤَكِّدُونَ	أَكَّدْتَ / أَكَّدْتُمَا / أَكَّدْتُمْ	أَنْتَ / أَنْتُمَا / أَنْتُمْ
			أَكِّدِي / أَكِّدَا / أَكِّدْنَ	تُؤَكِّدِينَ / تُؤَكِّدَانِ / تُؤَكِّدْنَ	أَكَّدْتِ / أَكَّدْتُمَا / أَكَّدْتُنَّ	أَنْتِ / أَنْتُمَا / أَنْتُنَّ
				أُؤَكِّدُ / نُؤَكِّدُ	أَكَّدْتُ / أَكَّدْنَا	أَنَا / نَحْنُ

<u>Sentences</u>

أَكَّدْتُ مَوْعَدِي مَعْ الطَبِيبِ.1

أَكَّدْ مَكَانَكَ فِي الفَرِيقِ.2

يَجِبُ أَنْ تَتَأَكَّدَ مِن أَنْ تَغْسِلَ يَدَيكَ بَعْدَ الأَكْلِ.3

<u>English translation</u>

1. I confirmed my appointment with the doctor.
2. Affirm your position in the team.
3. You have to make sure that you wash your hands after eating.

Verb #52 – زَالَ – to disappear, to vanish, to cease
(When it comes with مَا before the verb, it means I am still)

اِسْم الْمَفْعُول (The passive participle)	اِسْم الْفَاعِل (The active participle)	الْمَصْدَر (Verbal Noun)	أَمْر (Imperative)	الْمُضَارِع (Present)	الْمَاضِي (Past)	الضَّمِير (pronoun)
مَزيل	زَائِل	زَيْل		يَزَالُ / يَزَالَانِ / يَزَالُونَ	زَالَ / زَالَا / زَالُوا	هُوَ / هُمَا / هُمْ
				تَزَالُ / تَزَالَانِ / يَزَلْنَ	زَالَتْ / زَالَتَا / زِلْنَ	هِيَ / هُمَا / هُنَّ
			زَلْ / زَالَا / زَالُوا	تَزَالُ / تَزَالَانِ / تَزَالُونَ	زِلْتَ / زِلْتُمَا / زِلْتُمْ	أَنْتَ / أَنْتُمَا / أَنْتُمْ
			زَالِي / زَالَا / زَلْنَ	تَزَالِينَ / تَزَالَانِ / تَزَلْنَ	زِلْتِ / زِلْتُمَا / زِلْتُنَّ	أَنْتِ / أَنْتُمَا / أَنْتُنَّ
				أَزَالُ / نَزَالُ	زِلْتُ / زِلْنَا	أَنَا / نَحْنُ

<u>Sentences</u>

١. مَا زِلْتُ جَاهِلاً فِي الفِيزِيَاء

٢. زَالَ الثُرَابَ مِن قَمِيصِي

٣. زَالَ مِنْ وَجْهِ هَذِهِ الأَرْضِ

English translation

1. I am still bad at physics.
2. The dust disappeared from my shirt.
3. He vanished from the face of this earth.

Verb #53 – عَنَى – to mean, to signify

اِسْم الْمَفْعُول (The passive participle)	اِسْم الْفَاعِل (The active participle)	الْمَصْدَر (Verbal Noun)	أَمْرٌ (Imperative)	الْمُضَارِع (Present)	الْمَاضِي (Past)	الضَّمِير (Pronoun)
مَعْنِيّ	عَانٍ	عَنْى		يَعْنِي يَعْنِيَانِ يَعْنُونَ	عَنَى عَنَيَا عَنَوْا	هُوَ هُمَا هُمْ
				تَعْنِي تَعْنِيَانِ يَعْنِينَ	عَنَتْ عَنَيَا عَنَيْنَ	هِيَ هُمَا هُنَّ
			اِعْنِ اِعْنِيَا اِعْنُوا	تَعْنِي تَعْنِيَانِ تَعْنُونَ	عَنَيْتَ عَنَيْتُمَا عَنَيْتُمْ	أَنْتَ أَنْتُمَا أَنْتُمْ
			اِعْنِي اِعْنِيَا اِعْنِينَ	تَعْنِينَ تَعْنِيَانِ تَعْنِينَ	عَنَيْتِ عَنَيْتُمَا عَنَيْتُنَّ	أَنْتِ أَنْتُمَا أَنْتُنَّ
				أَعْنِي نَعْنِي	عَنَيْتُ عَنَيْنَا	أَنَا نَحْنُ

Sentences

مَاذَا تَعْنِي؟ 1.

لا يَعْنِي ذَلِكَ شيئًا! 2.

مَاذَا تَعْنِي بِإِشَارَات يَدَكَ؟ 3.

English translation

1. What do you mean?
2. That doesn't mean anything!
3. What do you mean with your hand gestures?

Verb #54 – حَمَلَ – to carry, to bring

إِسْم الْمَفْعُول (The passive participle)	إِسْم الْفَاعِل (The active participle)	الْمَصْدَر (Verbal Noun)	أَمْرٌ (Imperative)	الْمُضَارِع (Present)	الْمَاضِي (Past)	الضَّمِير (pronoun)
مَحْمُول	حَامِل	حَمْل		يَحْمِلُ يَحْمِلَانِ يَحْمِلُونَ	حَمَلَ حَمَلَا حَمَلُوا	هُوَ هُمَا هُمْ
				تَحْمِلُ تَحْمِلَانِ يَحْمِلْنَ	حَمَلَتْ حَمَلَتَا حَمَلْنَ	هِيَ هُمَا هُنَّ
			اِحْمِلْ اِحْمِلَا اِحْمِلُوا	تَحْمِلُ تَحْمِلَانِ تَحْمِلُونَ	حَمَلْتَ حَمَلْتُمَا حَمَلْتُمْ	أَنْتَ أَنْتُمَا أَنْتُمْ
			اِحْمِلِي اِحْمِلَا اِحْمِلْنَ	تَحْمِلِينَ تَحْمِلَانِ تَحْمِلْنَ	حَمَلْتِ حَمَلْتُمَا حَمَلْتُنَّ	أَنْتِ أَنْتُمَا أَنْتُنَّ
				أَحْمِلُ نَحْمِلُ	حَمَلْتُ حَمَلْنَا	أَنَا نَحْنُ

Sentences

1. حَمَلَتْكَ أُمَّكَ فِي رَحِمَهَا لِمُدَّةٍ تِسْعَةً أَشْهُرٍ.

2. اِحْمِلْ مَعَكَ دَفْتَرَ مُلَاحَظَاتِكَ اِلى الصَّفِ.

3. لَا تَحْمِلِ أَعْبَاءَ الآخَرِينَ مَعَكَ.

English translation

1. Your mother carried you in her womb for nine months.
2. Carry your notebook with you to class.
3. Do not carry the burden of other people with you.

Verb #55 – خَرَجَ - to go out, to exit

اِسْم الْمَفْعُول (The passive participle)	اِسْم الْفَاعِل (The active participle)	الْمَصْدَر (Verbal Noun)	أَمْرٌ (Imperative)	الْمُضَارِع (Present)	الْمَاضِي (Past)	الضَّمِير (pronoun)
مَخْرُوج	خَارِج	خُرُوج		يَخْرُجُ يَخْرُجَانِ يَخْرُجُونَ	خَرَجَ خَرَجَا خَرَجُوا	هُوَ هُمَا هُمْ
				تَخْرُجُ تَخْرُجَانِ يَخْرُجْنَ	خَرَجَتْ خَرَجَتَا خَرَجْنَ	هِيَ هُمَا هُنَّ
			أُخْرُجْ أُخْرُجَا أُخْرُجُوا	تَخْرُجُ تَخْرُجَانِ تَخْرُجُونَ	خَرَجْتَ خَرَجْتُمَا خَرَجْتُمْ	أَنْتَ أَنْتُمَا أَنْتُمْ
			أُخْرُجِي أُخْرُجَا أُخْرُجْنَ	تَخْرُجِينَ تَخْرُجَانِ تَخْرُجْنَ	خَرَجْتِ خَرَجْتُمَا خَرَجْتُنَّ	أَنْتِ أَنْتُمَا أَنْتُنَّ
				أَخْرُجُ نَخْرُجُ	خَرَجْتُ خَرَجْنَا	أَنَا نَحْنُ

Sentences

1. خَرَجْتُ مِن المَتْحَفِ
2. لا تَخْرُجْ مِن الإجْتِمَاعِ
3. خَرَجَتْ فَاطِمَةُ مِن بَيتِها غَاضِبَةً

English translation

1. I came out/exited the museum.
2. Do not leave the meeting.
3. Fatima left her house angry.

Verb #56 – وَضَعَ – to put, to place, to set

اِسْم الْمَفْعُول (The passive participle)	اِسْم الْفَاعِل (The active participle)	الْمَصْدَر (Verbal Noun)	أَمْرّ (Imperative)	الْمُضَارِع (Present)	الْمَاضِي (Past)	الضَّمِير (pronoun)
مَوْضُوع	وَاضِع	وَضْع		يَضَعُ / يَضَعَانِ / يَضَعُونَ	وَضَعَ / وَضَعَا / وَضَعُوا	هُوَ / هُمَا / هُمْ
				تَضَعُ / تَضَعَانِ / يَضَعْنَ	وَضَعَتْ / وَضَعَتَا / وَضَعْنَ	هِيَ / هُمَا / هُنَّ
			ضَعْ / ضَعَا / ضَعُوا	تَضَعُ / تَضَعَانِ / تَضَعُونَ	وَضَعْتَ / وَضَعْتُمَا / وَضَعْتُمْ	أَنْتَ / أَنْتُمَا / أَنْتُمْ
			ضَعِي / ضَعَا / ضَعْنَ	تَضَعِينَ / تَضَعَانِ / تَضَعْنَ	وَضَعْتِ / وَضَعْتُمَا / وَضَعْتُنَّ	أَنْتِ / أَنْتُمَا / أَنْتُنَّ
				أَضَعُ / نَضَعُ	وَضَعْتُ / وَضَعْنَا	أَنَا / نَحْنُ

Sentences

1. وَضَعْتُ قَلَمِي في جَيْبِي

2. وَضَعْتُ الْجِهَازَ في الطَّابِقِ ثُمَّ اِنْطَلَقْتُ

3. عَلَيْنَا اَنْ نَضَعَ بَعْضَ الحُدُود

English translation

1. I put my pen in my pocket.
2. I placed the device on the floor and then I walked away.
3. It is upon us to set some boundaries.

Verb #57 – عَلِمَ – to know, to learn, to realize

اِسْم الْمَفْعُول (The passive participle)	اِسْم الْفَاعِل (The active participle)	الْمَصْدَر (Verbal Noun)	أَمْرٌ (Imperative)	الْمُضَارِع (Present)	الْمَاضِى (Past)	الضَّمِير (Pronoun)
مَعْلُوم	عَالِم	عِلْم		يَعْلَمُ يَعْلَمَانِ يَعْلَمُونَ	عَلِمَ عَلِمَا عَلِمُوا	هُوَ هُمَا هُمْ
				تَعْلَمُ تَعْلَمَانِ يَعْلَمْنَ	عَلِمَتْ عَلِمَتَا عَلِمْنَ	هِيَ هُمَا هُنَّ
			اِعْلَمْ اِعْلَمَا اِعْلَمُوا	تَعْلَمُ تَعْلَمَانِ تَعْلَمُونَ	عَلِمْتَ عَلِمْتُمَا عَلِمْتُمْ	أَنْتَ أَنْتُمَا أَنْتُمْ
			اِعْلَمِي اِعْلَمَا اِعْلَمْنَ	تَعْلَمِينَ تَعْلَمَانِ تَعْلَمْنَ	عَلِمْتِ عَلِمْتُمَا عَلِمْتُنَّ	أَنْتِ أَنْتُمَا أَنْتُنَّ
				أَعْلَمُ نَعْلَمُ	عَلِمْتُ عَلِمْنَا	أَنَا نَحْنُ

Sentences

١. لا أَرْغَبُ فِي دِرَاسَةِ عِلْمُ الفَلْسَفَةِ.

٢. اِعْلَمْ أَنَّ الآلَمَ مُؤقَّتَ

٣. فَلَمَّا عَلِمْتُ أَنَّكَ عَدُوٌّ لِي، اِبْتَعَدْتُ عَنْكَ

English translation

1. I have no intrest in studying philosophy.
2. Know that pain is temporary.
3. When I realised that you were an enemy to me, I moved away from you.

Verb #58 – أَمِنَ – to be safe, to be secure

اِسْم الْمَفْعُول (The passive participle)	اِسْم الْفَاعِل (The active participle)	الْمَصْدَر (Verbal Noun)	أَمْر (Imperative)	الْمُضَارِع (Present)	الْمَاضِي (Past)	الضّمِير (pronoun)
مَأْمُون	آمِن	أَمْن		يَأْمَنُ / يَأْمَنَانِ / يَأْمَنُونَ	أَمِنَ / أَمِنَا / أَمِنُوا	هُوَ / هُمَا / هُمْ
				تَأْمَنُ / تَأْمَنَانِ / يَأْمَنَّ	أَمِنَتْ / أَمِنَتَا / أَمِنَّ	هِيَ / هُمَا / هُنَّ
			اِيمَنْ / اِيمَنَا / اِيمَنُوا	تَأْمَنُ / تَأْمَنَانِ / تَأْمَنُونَ	أَمِنْتَ / أَمِنْتُمَا / أَمِنْتُمْ	أَنْتَ / أَنْتُمَا / أَنْتُمْ
			اِيمَنِي / اِيمَنَا / اِيمَنَّ	تَأْمَنِينَ / تَأْمَنَانِ / تَأْمَنَّ	أَمِنْتِ / أَمِنْتُمَا / أَمِنْتُنَّ	أَنْتِ / أَنْتُمَا / أَنْتُنَّ
				آمَنُ / نَأْمَنُ	أَمِنْتُ / أَمِنَّا	أَنَا / نَحْنُ

Sentences

1.؟أَفَاَمِنُو مِن الْكَارِثَةِ الطَّبِيعِيَّةِ

2.كُلُّ شَخْصٍ يَسْتَحِقُّ الْحَقَّ فِي الْأَمْنِ

3.؟أَلَا تَشْعُرُ بِالْأَمْنِ

English translation

1. Do they feel safe/secure from the natural disaster?
2. Everybody deserves the right to security.
3. Do you not feel safe?

Verb #59 – حَدَثَ – to happen, occur, take place

اِسْم الْمَفْعُول (The passive participle)	اِسْم الْفَاعِل (The active participle)	الْمَصْدَر (Verbal Noun)	أَمْرٌ (Imperative)	الْمُضَارع (Present)	الْمَاضِي (Past)	الضّمِير (pronoun)
مَحْدُوث	حَادِث	حُدُوث		يَحْدُث / يَحْدُثَان / يَحْدُثُونَ	حَدَثَ / حَدَثَا / حَدَثُوا	هُوَ / هُمَا / هُمْ
				تَحْدُث / تَحْدُثَان / يَحْدُثْنَ	حَدَثَتْ / حَدَثَتَا / حَدَثْنَ	هِيَ / هُمَا / هُنَّ
			أُحْدُث / أُحْدُثَا / أُحْدُثُوا	تَحْدُث / تَحْدُثَان / تَحْدُثُونَ	حَدَثْتَ / حَدَثْتُمَا / حَدَثْتُمْ	أَنْتَ / أَنْتُمَا / أَنْتُمْ
			أُحْدُثِي / أُحْدُثَا / أُحْدُثْنَ	تَحْدُثِينَ / تَحْدُثَان / تَحْدُثْنَ	حَدَثْتِ / حَدَثْتُمَا / حَدَثْتُنَّ	أَنْتِ / أَنْتُمَا / أَنْتُنَّ
				أَحْدُث / نَحْدُث	حَدَثْتُ / حَدَثْنَا	أَنَا / نَحْنُ

Sentences

1.؟مَاذَا حَدَثَ بِكَ؟

2.حُدُوث فَيرُوْس كَرَوْنَا أَفْسَدَ عَامِنَا

3.؟هَلْ تَعْرِفُ مَاذَا حَدَثَ بِالامْس؟

English translation

1. What happened to you?
2. The occurance of coronavirus has ruined our year.
3. Do you know what happened/occured yesterday?

Verb #60 – اِعْتَقَدَ – to believe, to think, to suppose

اِسْم الْمَفْعُول (The passive participle)	اِسْم الْفَاعِل (The active participle)	الْمَصْدَر (Verbal Noun)	أَمْر (Imperative)	الْمُضَارِع (Present)	الْمَاضِي (Past)	الضَّمِير (Pronoun)
مُعْتَقَد	مُعْتَقِد	اِعْتِقَاد		يَعْتَقِدُ / يَعْتَقِدَانِ / يَعْتَقِدُونَ	اِعْتَقَدَ / اِعْتَقَدَا / اِعْتَقَدُوا	هُوَ / هُمَا / هُمْ
				تَعْتَقِدُ / تَعْتَقِدَانِ / يَعْتَقِدْنَ	اِعْتَقَدَتْ / اِعْتَقَدَتَا / اِعْتَقَدْنَ	هِيَ / هُمَا / هُنَّ
			اِعْتَقِدْ / اِعْتَقِدَا / اِعْتَقِدُوا	تَعْتَقِدُ / تَعْتَقِدَانِ / تَعْتَقِدُونَ	اِعْتَقَدْتَ / اِعْتَقَدْتُمَا / اِعْتَقَدْتُمْ	أَنْتَ / أَنْتُمَا / أَنْتُمْ
			اِعْتَقِدِي / اِعْتَقِدَا / اِعْتَقِدْنَ	تَعْتَقِدِينَ / تَعْتَقِدَانِ / يَعْتَقِدْنَ	اِعْتَقَدْتِ / اِعْتَقَدْتُمَا / اِعْتَقَدْتُنَّ	أَنْتِ / أَنْتُمَا / أَنْتُنَّ
				أَعْتَقِدُ / نَعْتَقِدُ	اِعْتَقَدْتُ / اِعْتَقَدْنَا	أَنَا / نَحْنُ

Sentences

1.؟مَاذَا تَعْتَقِدُ في العَقِيدَة

2.أَعْتَقِدُ أَنَّكَ جَاهِلً

3.أَعْتَقِدُ أَنَّنا سَنَكْتَشِفُ الحَقِيقة

English translation

1. What are your beliefs in creed?
2. I think you are ignorant.
3. I suppose we will find out the truth.

Verb #61 – أَعْلَنَ – to announce, declare, to state

إِسْم الْمَفْعُول (The passive participle)	إِسْم الْفَاعِل (The active participle)	الْمَصْدَر (Verbal Noun)	أَمْرٌ (Imperative)	الْمُضَارع (Present)	الْمَاضِى (Past)	الضَّمِير (Pronoun)
مُعْلَن	مُعْلِن	إِعْلَان		يُعْلِنُ يُعْلِنَان يُعْلِنُونَ	أَعْلَنَ أَعْلَنَا أَعْلَنُوا	هُوَ هُمَا هُمْ
				تُعْلِنُ تُعْلِنَان تُعْلِنَّ	أَعْلَنَتْ أَعْلَنَتَا أَعْلَنَّ	هِيَ هُمَا هُنَّ
			أَعْلِنْ أَعْلِنَا أَعْلِنُوا	تُعْلِنُ تُعْلِنَان تُعْلِنُونَ	أَعْلَنْتَ أَعْلَنْتُمَا أَعْلَنْتُمْ	أَنْتَ أَنْتُمَا أَنْتُمْ
			أَعْلِنِي أَعْلِنَا أَعْلِنَّ	تُعْلِنِينَ تُعْلِنَان تُعْلِنَّ	أَعْلَنْتِ أَعْلَنْتُمَا أَعْلَنْتُنَّ	أَنْتِ أَنْتُمَا أَنْتُنَّ
				أُعْلِنُ نُعْلِنُ	أَعْلَنْتُ أَعْلَنَّا	أَنَا نَحْنُ

Sentences

١. أَعْلَنَ أَنَّ زَوْجَتَهُ حَامِل

٢. أَعْلِنتْ الحَرْبُ

٣. أَعْلَنَ الرَجُلُ أَنّه سَيَغْتَرِبُ اِلى الصِين

English translation

1. He announced that his wife is pregnant.
2. A ware was declared.
3. The man announced that he is going to move to china.

Verb #62 – بَلَغَ – to reach

اِسْم الْمَفْعُول (The passive participle)	اِسْم الْفَاعِل (The active participle)	الْمَصْدَر (Verbal Noun)	أَمْر (Imperative)	الْمُضَارِع (Present)	الْمَاضِي (Past)	الضَّمِير (pronoun)
مَبْلُوغ	بَالغ	بُلُوغ		يَبْلُغُ بَلَغَتَا يَبْلُغُونَ	بَلَغَ بَلَغَا بَلَغُوا	هُوَ هُمَا هُمْ
				تَبْلُغُ تَبْلُغَانِ يَبْلُغْنَ	بَلَغَتْ بَلَغَتَا بَلَغْنَ	هِيَ هُمَا هُنَّ
			أُبْلُغْ أُبْلُغَا أُبْلُغُوا	تَبْلُغُ تَبْلُغَانِ تَبْلُغُونَ	بَلَغْتَ بَلَغْتُمَا بَلَغْتُمْ	أَنْتَ أَنْتُمَا أَنْتُمْ
			أُبْلُغِي أُبْلُغَا أُبْلُغْنَ	تَبْلُغِينَ تَبْلُغَانِ تَبْلُغْنَ	بَلَغْتِ بَلَغْتُمَا بَلَغْتُنَّ	أَنْتِ أَنْتُمَا أَنْتُنَّ
				أَبْلُغُ نَبْلُغُ	بَلَغْتُ بَلَغْنَا	أَنَا نَحْنُ

Sentences

1. بَلَغْتُ العِشْرُونَ مِن عُمْري

2. أَمْبَر بَلَغَتْ سِنَّ البُلُوغ

3. بَلَغَ فَريقِي لِكُرَّةِ القَدَمِ اِلى النِهَائِي

English translation

1. I have reached 20 in age.

2. Amber has reached the age of puberty.

3. My football team has reached the final.

Verb #63 أدّى – to lead, to perform (Comes with إلى)

اِسْم الْمَفْعُول (The passive participle)	اِسْم الْفَاعِل (The active participle)	الْمَصْدَر (Verbal Noun)	أَمْر (Imperative)	الْمُضَارِع (Present)	الْمَاضِي (Past)	الضَّمِير (pronoun)
مُؤَدَّى	مُؤَدٍّ	أَدَاء		يُؤَدِّي / يُؤَدِّيَانِ / يُؤَدُّونَ	أَدَّى / أَدَّيَا / أَدُّوا	هُوَ / هُمَا / هُمْ
				تُؤَدِّي / تُؤَدِّيَانِ / يُؤَدِّينَ	أَدَّتْ / أَدَّتَا / أَدَّيْنَ	هِيَ / هُمَا / هُنَّ
			أَدِّ / أَدِّيَا / أَدُّوا	تُؤَدِّي / تُؤَدِّيَانِ / تُؤَدُّونَ	أَدَّيْتَ / أَدَّيْتُمَا / أَدَّيْتُمْ	أَنْتَ / أَنْتُمَا / أَنْتُمْ
			أَدِّي / أَدِّيَا / أَدِّينَ	تُؤَدِّينَ / تُؤَدِّيَانِ / تُؤَدِّينَ	أَدَّيْتِ / أَدَّيْتُمَا / أَدَّيْتُنَّ	أَنْتِ / أَنْتُمَا / أَنْتُنَّ
				أُؤَدِّي / نُؤَدِّي	أَدَّيْتُ / أَدَّيْنَا	أَنَا / نَحْنُ

Sentences

1. أَبْدَأُ اليَوْمَ بِأَدَاءِ الصَّلَاةِ

2. الإِجْهَاد يُؤدِي اِلى فِقْدَانِ الشَّعْرِ

3. أَدَّتْ تِلْكَ التَجْرِبَةُ اِلى نِماءٍ

English translation

1. I start the day by performing the prayer.
2. Stress leads to hair loss.
3. That experience led to experience.

Verb #64 – رَدَّ – to return, to respond

اِسْم الْمَفْعُول (The passive participle)	اِسْم الْفَاعِل (The active participle)	الْمَصْدَر (Verbal Noun)	أَمْر (Imperative)	الْمُضَارِع (Present)	الْمَاضِي (Past)	الضَّمِير (pronoun)
مَرْدُود	رَادّ	رَدّ		يَرُدُّ / يَرُدَّانِ / يَرُدُّونَ	رَدَّ / رَدَّا / رَدُّوا	هُوَ / هُمَا / هُمْ
				تَرُدُّ / تَرُدَّانِ / يَرْدُدْنَ	رَدَّتْ / رَدَّتَا / رَدَدْنَ	هِيَ / هُمَا / هُنَّ
			رُدَّ / رُدَّا / رُدُّوا	تَرُدُّ / تَرُدَّانِ / تَرُدُّونَ	رَدَدْتَ / رَدَدْتُمَا / رَدَدْتُمْ	أَنْتَ / أَنْتُمَا / أَنْتُمْ
			رُدِّي / رُدَّا / ارْدُدْنَ	تَرُدِّينَ / تَرُدَّانِ / تَرُدُّدْنَ	رَدَدْتِ / رَدَدْتُمَا / رَدَدْتُنَّ	أَنْتِ / أَنْتُمَا / أَنْتُنَّ
				أَرُدُّ / نَرُدُّ	رَدَدْتُ / رَدَدْنَا	أَنَا / نَحْنُ

Sentences

١. لا تَرُدَّ اِلى السُفَهَاءِ

٢. سَأُرُدُّ مِن العُطْلَةِ هَذَا الأَسْبُوع

٣. رُدَّ المَال الذي أَخَذْتُهُ

English translation

1. Do not respond to the foolish people.
2. I will be returning from holiday this week.
3. Return the money that you took.

Verb #65 – ذَكَرَ – to recall, to mention, to remember

اِسْم الْمَفْعُول (The passive participle)	اِسْم الْفَاعِل (The active participle)	الْمَصْدَر (Verbal Noun)	أَمْرٌ (Imperative)	الْمُضَارِع (Present)	الْمَاضِي (Past)	الضَّمِير (pronoun)
مَذْكُور	ذَاكِر	ذِكْر		يَذْكُر يَذْكُرَانِ يَذْكُرُونَ	ذَكَرَ ذَكَرَا ذَكَرُوا	هُوَ هُمَا هُمْ
				تَذْكُر تَذْكُرَانِ يَذْكُرْنَ	ذَكَرَتْ ذَكَرَتَا ذَكَرْنَ	هِيَ هُمَا هُنَّ
			أُذْكُرْ أُذْكُرَا أُذْكُرُوا	تَذْكُر تَذْكُرَانِ تَذْكُرُونَ	ذَكَرْتَ ذَكَرْتُمَا ذَكَرْتُمْ	أَنْتَ أَنْتُمَا أَنْتُمْ
			أُذْكُرِي أُذْكُرَا أُذْكُرْنَ	تَذْكُرِينَ تَذْكُرَانِ تَذْكُرْنَ	ذَكَرْتِ ذَكَرْتُمَا ذَكَرْتُنَّ	أَنْتِ أَنْتُمَا أَنْتُنَّ
				أَذْكُرُ نَذْكُرُ	ذَكَرْتُ ذَكَرْنَا	أَنَا نَحْنُ

Sentences

1.أَذْكُرُ عِنْدَمَا حَلَقْتُ شَعَرِي الاسْبُوع المَاضِي

2.هَلْ يُمْكِنُكَ أَنْ تَذْكُرَ عِنْدَمَا كُنْتَ طِفْلاً

3.اُذْكُرْنِي فِي دُعَائِكَ مِنْ فَضْلِكَ

English translation

1. I remember when I shaved my hair last week.

2. Are you able to recall when you were a child?

3. Mention me in your supplications, please.

Verb #66 – دَخَلَ – to enter

اِسْم الْمَفْعُول (The passive participle)	اِسْم الْفَاعِل (The active participle)	الْمَصْدَر (Verbal Noun)	أَمْرٌ (Imperative)	الْمُضَارِع (Present)	الْمَاضِي (Past)	الضَّمِير (pronoun)
مَدْخُول	دَاخِل	دُخُول		يَدْخُلُ يَدْخُلَانِ يَدْخُلُونَ	دَخَلَ دَخَلَا دَخَلُوا	هُوَ هُمَا هُمْ
				تَدْخُلُ تَدْخُلَانِ يَدْخُلْنَ	دَخَلَتْ دَخَلَتَا دَخَلْنَ	هِيَ هُمَا هُنَّ
			أُدْخُلْ أُدْخُلَا أُدْخُلُوا	تَدْخُلُ تَدْخُلَانِ تَدْخُلُونَ	دَخَلْتَ دَخَلْتُمَا دَخَلْتُمْ	أَنْتَ أَنْتُمَا أَنْتُمْ
			أُدْخُلِي أُدْخُلَا أُدْخُلْنَ	تَدْخُلِينَ تَدْخُلَانِ تَدْخُلْنَ	دَخَلْتِ دَخَلْتُمَا دَخَلْتُنَّ	أَنْتِ أَنْتُمَا أَنْتُنَّ
				أَدْخُلُ نَدْخُلُ	دَخَلْتُ دَخَلْنَا	أَنَا نَحْنُ

<u>Sentences</u>

1.اُدْخُلْ المَنْزِلَ بدُوْنَ حَذَائِكَ

2.لا يَسْمَحُ لَكَ الدُخُولَ في هَذَا الوَقْتِ

3.دَخَلُوا النَّاسُ الكَنِيسَةَ

<u>English translation</u>

1. Enter the house without your shoes.
2. You are not allowed to enter at this time.
3. The people have entered the church.

Verb #67 – أَضَافَ – to add

اِسْم الْمَفْعُول (The passive participle)	اِسْم الْفَاعِل (The active participle)	الْمَصْدَر (Verbal Noun)	أَمْرٌ (Imperative)	الْمُضَارِع (Present)	الْمَاضِي (Past)	الضَّمِير (pronoun)
مُضَاف	مُضِيف	إِضَافَة		يُضِيفُ يُضِيفَانِ يُضِيفُونَ	أَضَافَ أَضَافَا أَضَافُوا	هُوَ هُمَا هُمْ
				تُضِيفُ تُضِيفَانِ يُضِفْنَ	أَضَافَتْ أَضَافَتَا أَضَفْنَ	هِيَ هُمَا هُنَّ
			أَضِفْ أَضِيفَا أَضِيفُوا	تُضِيفُ تُضِيفَانِ تُضِيفُونَ	أَضَفْتَ أَضَفْتُمَا أَضَفْتُمْ	أَنْتَ أَنْتُمَا أَنْتُمْ
			أَضِيفِي أَضِيفَا أَضِفْنَ	تُضِيفِينَ تُضِيفَانِ تُضِفْنَ	أَضَفْتِ أَضَفْتُمَا أَضَفْتُنَّ	أَنْتِ أَنْتُمَا أَنْتُنَّ
				أُضِيفُ نُضِيفُ	أَضَفْتُ أَضَفْنَا	أَنَا نَحْنُ

Sentences

1. هَلْ يُمْكِنُكَ أَنْ تُضِيفُ المُكَوِّنات التي نَحْتَاجُحَا؟

2. إِذَا أَضْفتَ كُلَّ أَصْدِقَائَكَ الحَقِيقِينَ، سَتَجِدُهُم قَلِيلون

3. أَنَا لَسْتُ بِجَيِّد فِي إِضَافَةِ الأَرْقَامِ

English translation

1. Can you add all of the ingredients that we need?
2. If you add up all of your real friends, you will find them little.
3. I'm not very good at adding numbers.

Verb #68 – سَأَلَ – to ask, inquire, request

اِسْم الْمَفْعُول (The passive participle)	اِسْم الْفَاعِل (The active participle)	الْمَصْدَر (Verbal Noun)	أَمْرٌ (Imperative)	الْمُضَارِع (Present)	الْمَاضِي (Past)	الضَّمِير (pronoun)
مَسْؤُول	سَائِل	سُؤَال		يَسْأَلُ يَسْأَلَانِ يَسْأَلُونَ	سَأَلَ سَأَلَا سَأَلُوا	هُوَ هُمَا هُمْ
				تَسْأَلُ تَسْأَلَانِ يَسْأَلْنَ	سَأَلَتْ سَأَلَتَا سَأَلْنَ	هِيَ هُمَا هُنَّ
			اِسْأَلْ اِسْأَلَا اِسْأَلُوا	تَسْأَلُ تَسْأَلَانِ تَسْأَلُونَ	سَأَلْتَ سَأَلْتُمَا سَأَلْتُمْ	أَنْتَ أَنْتُمَا أَنْتُمْ
			اِسْأَلِي اِسْأَلَا اِسْأَلْنَ	تَسْأَلِينَ تَسْأَلَانِ تَسْأَلْنَ	سَأَلْتِ سَأَلْتُمَا سَأَلْتُنَّ	أَنْتِ أَنْتُمَا أَنْتُنَّ
				أَسْأَلُ نَسْأَلُ	سَأَلْتُ سَأَلْنَا	أَنَا نَحْنُ

<u>Sentences</u>

1.إِذَا كُنْتَ لَا تَعْرِفُ، اِسْأَلْ الْمُعَلِّمَ

2.لا تَسْأَلْ عَمَّا لا يَعْنِيكَ

3.لِمَاذَا تَسْأَلُونَ عَن الامر؟

<u>English translation</u>

1. If you do not know, then ask the teacher.
2. Do not ask about what does not concern you.
3. Why are you asking about the matter?

Verb #69 – سَلَّمَ – to greet, to hand something over, to deliver

إِسْم الْمَفْعُول (The passive participle)	إِسْم الْفَاعِل (The active participle)	الْمَصْدَر (Verbal Noun)	أَمْرٌ (Imperative)	الْمُضَارِع (Present)	الْمَاضِي (Past)	الضَّمِير (pronoun)
مُسَلَّم	مُسَلِّم	تَسْلِيم		يُسَلِّمُ / يُسَلِّمَانِ / يُسَلِّمُونَ	سَلَّمَ / سَلَّمَا / سَلَّمُوا	هُوَ / هُمَا / هُمْ
				تُسَلِّمُ / تُسَلِّمَانِ / يُسَلِّمْنَ	سَلَّمَتْ / سَلَّمَتَا / سَلَّمْنَ	هِيَ / هُمَا / هُنَّ
			سَلِّمْ / سَلِّمَا / سَلِّمُوا	تُسَلِّمُ / تُسَلِّمَانِ / تُسَلِّمُونَ	سَلَّمْتَ / سَلَّمْتُمَا / سَلَّمْتُمْ	أَنْتَ / أَنْتُمَا / أَنْتُمْ
			سَلِّمِي / سَلِّمَا / سَلِّمْنَ	تُسَلِّمِينَ / تُسَلِّمَانِ / تُسَلِّمْنَ	سَلَّمْتِ / سَلَّمْتُمَا / سَلَّمْتُنَّ	أَنْتِ / أَنْتُمَا / أَنْتُنَّ
				أُسَلِّمُ / نُسَلِّمُ	سَلَّمْتُ / سَلَّمْنَا	أَنَا / نَحْنُ

Sentences

1. سَلَّمْتُ وَاجِبَاتِي إِلى الْمُدَرِّسُ

2. سَلَّمَنِي رَجُل التَّسْلِيم الطُّرُودَ

3. سَلِّمْ عَلى أَبِيكَ لِي

English translation

1. I handed over my homework to the teacher.
2. The delivery man handed me over the parcel.
3. Send my greetings to your father for me.

Verb #70 – عَاشَ – to live, to reside

اِسْم الْمَفْعُول (The passive participle)	اِسْم الْفَاعِل (The active participle)	الْمَصْدَر (Verbal Noun)	أَمْرٌ (Imperative)	الْمُضَارِع (Present)	الْمَاضِي (Past)	الضَّمِير (pronoun)
مَعِيش	عَائِش	عَيْش		يَعِيشُ / يَعِيشَانِ / يَعِيشُونَ	عَاشَ / عَاشَا / عَاشُوا	هُوَ / هُمَا / هُمْ
				تَعِيشُ / تَعِيشَانِ / يَعِشْنَ	عَاشَتْ / عَاشَتَا / عِشْنَ	هِيَ / هُمَا / هُنَّ
			عِشْ / عِيشَا / عِيشُوا	تَعِيشُ / تَعِيشَانِ / تَعِيشُونَ	عِشْتَ / عِشْتُمَا / عِشْتُمْ	أَنْتَ / أَنْتُمَا / أَنْتُمْ
			عِيشِي / عِيشَا / عِشْنَ	تَعِيشِينَ / تَعِيشَانِ / تَعِشْنَ	عِشْتِ / عِشْتُمَا / عِشْتُنَّ	أَنْتِ / أَنْتُمَا / أَنْتُنَّ
				أَعِيشُ / نَعِيشُ	عِشْتُ / عِشْنَا	أَنَا / نَحْنُ

<u>Sentences</u>

عِشْتُ فِي لَنْدَن لِمُدَّةِ سَنَتَين .1
العَيْشُ فِي أُورُوبا أَفْضَلُ مِن هُنا.2
أُرِيدُ العَيْشَ فِي إِسْبَانْيَا.3

<u>English translation</u>

1. I have lived in london for two years now.
2. Living in Europe is better than living here.
3. I want to reside/live in Spain.

Verb #71 – وَجَبَ – to be necessary, obligatory (comes with عَلَى)

اِسْم الْمَفْعُول (The passive participle)	اِسْم الْفَاعِل (The active participle)	الْمَصْدَر (Verbal Noun)	أَمْر (Imperative)	الْمُضَارِع (Present)	الْمَاضِي (Past)	الضَّمِير (pronoun)
مَوْجُوب	وَاجِب	وُجُوب		يَجِبُ يَجِبَانِ يَجِبُونَ	وَجَبَ وَجَبَا وَجَبُوا	هُوَ هُمَا هُمْ
				تَجِبُ تَجِبَانِ يَجِبْنَ	وَجَبَتْ وَجَبَتَا وَجَبْنَ	هِيَ هُمَا هُنَّ
			جِبْ جِبَا جِبُوا	تَجِبُ تَجِبَانِ تَجِبُونَ	وَجَبْتَ وَجَبْتُمَا وَجَبْتُمْ	أَنْتَ أَنْتُمَا أَنْتُمْ
			جِي جِبَا جِئْنَ	تَجِبِينَ تَجِبَانِ تَجِبْنَ	وَجَبْتِ وَجَبْتُمَا وَجَبْتُنَّ	أَنْتِ أَنْتُمَا أَنْتُنَّ
				أَجِبُ نَجِبُ	وَجَبْتُ وَجَبْنَا	أَنَا نَحْنُ

Sentences

1.وَجَبَ عَلَيْنَا الصَلَاة

2.يَجِبُ عَلَيْنَا أَنْ نُرَاجِعَ لِلإِمْتِحَان

3.وَجَبَ عَلَيْهِم فِي تِلْكَ الْحَالَةِ

English translation

1. The prayer became obligatory upon us.
2. Its necessary upon us to revise for the exam.
3. It was obligatory for them in that case.

Verb #72 – وَقَعَ – to fall down, to happen, to occur

اِسْم الْمَفْعُول (The passive participle)	اِسْم الْفَاعِل (The active participle)	الْمَصْدَر (Verbal Noun)	أَمْرٌ (Imperative)	الْمُضَارِع (Present)	الْمَاضِي (Past)	الضَّمِير (pronoun)
مَوْقُوع	وَاقِع	وُقُوع		يَقَعُ / يَقَعَانِ / يَقَعُونَ	وَقَعَ / وَقَعَا / وَقَعُوا	هُوَ / هُمَا / هُمْ
				تَقَعُ / تَقَعَانِ / يَقَعْنَ	وَقَعَتْ / وَقَعَتَا / وَقَعْنَ	هِيَ / هُمَا / هُنَّ
			قَعْ / قَعَا / قَعُوا	تَقَعُ / تَقَعَانِ / تَقَعُونَ	وَقَعْتَ / وَقَعْتُمَا / وَقَعْتُمْ	أَنْتَ / أَنْتُمَا / أَنْتُمْ
			قَعِي / قَعَا / قَعْنَ	تَقَعِينَ / تَقَعَانِ / تَقَعْنَ	وَقَعْتِ / وَقَعْتُمَا / وَقَعْتُنَّ	أَنْتِ / أَنْتُمَا / أَنْتُنَّ
				أَقَعُ / نَقَعُ	وَقَعْتُ / وَقَعْنَا	أَنَا / نَحْنُ

<u>Sentences</u>

١.لِمَاذَا حَدَثَ بِنَا هَذَا؟
٢.وَقَعْتُ عَلى الْأَرْض
٣.وَقَعَ حَادِثٌ بِالأمسِ

<u>English translation</u>

1. Why did this happen to us?
2. I fell on the ground.
3. An accident occurred yesterday.

Verb #73 – حَصَلَ – to obtain, to happen

اِسْم الْمَفْعُول (The passive participle)	اِسْم الْفَاعِل (The active participle)	الْمَصْدَر (Verbal Noun)	أَمْرٌ (Imperative)	الْمُضَارِع (Present)	الْمَاضِي (Past)	الضَّمِير (pronoun)
مَحْصُول	حَاصِل	حُصُول		يَحْصُلُ / يَحْصُلَانِ / يَحْصُلُونَ	حَصَلَ / حَصَلَا / حَصَلُوا	هُوَ / هُمَا / هُمْ
				تَحْصُلُ / تَحْصُلَانِ / يَحْصُلْنَ	حَصَلَتْ / حَصَلَتَا / حَصَلْنَ	هِيَ / هُمَا / هُنَّ
			أُحْصُلْ / أُحْصُلَا / أُحْصُلُوا	تَحْصُلُ / تَحْصُلَانِ / تَحْصُلُونَ	حَصَلْتَ / حَصَلْتُمَا / حَصَلْتُمْ	أَنْتَ / أَنْتُمَا / أَنْتُمْ
			أُحْصُلِي / أُحْصُلَا / أُحْصُلْنَ	تَحْصُلِينَ / تَحْصُلَانِ / تَحْصُلْنَ	حَصَلْتِ / حَصَلْتُمَا / حَصَلْتُنَّ	أَنْتِ / أَنْتُمَا / أَنْتُنَّ
				أَحْصُلُ / نَحْصُلُ	حَصَلْتُ / حَصَلْنَا	أَنَا / نَحْنُ

<u>Sentences</u>

1. حَصَلْتُ عَلى دَرَجَةِ الإمْتِيَاز

2. مَاذَا حَصَلَ بِكَ؟

3. لِمَاذَا السَبَب عَلى حُصُوْلِ الطَلَاقِ صَعْبٌ؟

<u>English translation</u>

1. I obtainted an excellent grade.
2. What happened to you?
3. Why is it so hard to get a divorce?

Verb #74 – تَمَنَّى – to wish for, to hope for

اِسْم الْمَفْعُول (The passive participle)	اِسْم الْفَاعِل (The active participle)	الْمَصْدَر (Verbal Noun)	أَمْرٌ (Imperative)	الْمُضَارِع (Present)	الْمَاضِي (Past)	الضَّمِير (pronoun)
مُتَمَنَّى	مُتَمَنٍّ	تَمَنٍّ		يَتَمَنَّى / يَتَمَنَّيَانِ / يَتَمَنَّوْنَ	تَمَنَّى / تَمَنَّيَا / تَمَنَّوْا	هُوَ / هُمَا / هُمْ
				تَتَمَنَّى / تَتَمَنَّيَانِ / يَتَمَنَّيْنَ	تَمَنَّتْ / تَمَنَّتَا / تَمَنَّيْنَ	هِيَ / هُمَا / هُنَّ
			تَمَنَّ / تَمَنَّيَا / تَمَنَّوْا	تَتَمَنَّى / تَتَمَنَّيَانِ / تَتَمَنَّوْنَ	تَمَنَّيْتَ / تَمَنَّيْتُمَا / تَمَنَّيْتُمْ	أَنْتَ / أَنْتُمَا / أَنْتُمْ
			تَمَنَّيْ / تَمَنَّيَا / تَمَنَّيْنَ	تَتَمَنَّيْنَ / تَتَمَنَّيَانِ / تَتَمَنَّيْنَ	تَمَنَّيْتِ / تَمَنَّيْتُمَا / تَمَنَّيْتُنَّ	أَنْتِ / أَنْتُمَا / أَنْتُنَّ
				أَتَمَنَّى / نَتَمَنَّى	تَمَنَّيْتُ / تَمَنَّيْنَا	أَنَا / نَحْنُ

<u>Sentences</u>

1. لا أَتَمَنَّى لَكَ إِلَّا الخَيرِ.
2. أَتَمَنَّى أَنِّي سَأْنْجَحُ فِي الإِمْتِحَان.
3. نَتَمَنَّى أَنْ نَزُوْرَكُم قَرِيباً

<u>English translation</u>

1. I wish you nothing but good.
2. I hope that I will pass the test.
3. we hope to visit you soon.

Verb #75 – زَادَ – to increase

اِسْم الْمَفْعُول (The passive participle)	اِسْم الْفَاعِل (The active participle)	الْمَصْدَر (Verbal Noun)	أَمْرٌ (Imperative)	الْمُضَارِع (Present)	الْمَاضِي (Past)	الضَّمِير (pronoun)
مَزِيد	زَائِد	زِيَادَة		يَزِيدُ / يَزِيدَانِ / يَزِيدُونَ	زَادَ / زَادَا / زَادُوا	هُوَ / هُمَا / هُمْ
				تَزِيدُ / تَزِيدَانِ / يَزِدْنَ	زَادَتْ / زَادَتَا / زِدْنَ	هِيَ / هُمَا / هُنَّ
			زِدْ / زِيدَا / زِيدُوا	تَزِيدُ / تَزِيدَانِ / تَزِيدُونَ	زِدْتَ / زِدْتُمَا / زِدْتُمْ	أَنْتَ / أَنْتُمَا / أَنْتُمْ
			زِيدِي / زِيدَا / زِدْنَ	تَزِيدِينَ / تَزِيدَانِ / تَزِدْنَ	زِدْتِ / زِدْتُمَا / زِدْتُنَّ	أَنْتِ / أَنْتُمَا / أَنْتُنَّ
				أَزِيدُ / نَزِيدُ	زِدْتُ / زِدْنَا	أَنَا / نَحْنُ

<u>Sentences</u>

1. ‏لِمَاذَا زَادَ السِعْرَ؟
2. ‏ذَادَ حُبِّي لَكَ
3. ‏لِّلَّذِينَ أَحْسَنُوا الْحُسْنَىٰ وَزِيَادَةٌ (Quran, surah yunus verse 26)

<u>English translation</u>

1. Why did the price increase?
2. My love for you increased.
3. Those who do good will have the finest reward, and even more.

Verb #76 شَعَرَ – to feel, to be conscious

اِسْم الْمَفْعُول (The passive participle)	اِسْم الْفَاعِل (The active participle)	الْمَصْدَر (Verbal Noun)	أَمْرٌ (Imperative)	الْمُضَارِع (Present)	الْمَاضِي (Past)	الضَّمِير (pronoun)
مَشْعُور	شَاعِر	شُعُور		يَشْعُرُ / يَشْعُرَانِ / يَشْعُرُونَ	شَعَرَ / شَعَرَا / شَعَرُوا	هُوَ / هُمَا / هُمْ
				تَشْعُرُ / تَشْعُرَانِ / يَشْعُرْنَ	شَعَرَتْ / شَعَرَتَا / شَعَرْنَ	هِيَ / هُمَا / هُنَّ
			أُشْعُرْ / أُشْعُرَا / أُشْعُرُوا	تَشْعُرُ / تَشْعُرَانِ / تَشْعُرُونَ	شَعَرْتَ / شَعَرْتُمَا / شَعَرْتُمْ	أَنْتَ / أَنْتُمَا / أَنْتُمْ
			أُشْعُرِي / أُشْعُرَا / أُشْعُرْنَ	تَشْعُرِينَ / تَشْعُرَانِ / تَشْعُرْنَ	شَعَرْتِ / شَعَرْتُمَا / شَعَرْتُنَّ	أَنْتِ / أَنْتُمَا / أَنْتُنَّ
				أَشْعُرُ / نَشْعُرُ	شَعَرْتُ / شَعَرْنَا	أَنَا / نَحْنُ

<u>Sentences</u>

1. شَعَرْتُ بِأَلَمٍ فِي مَعِدَتِي
2. أَشْعُرُ بِالِامْتِنَانِ الشَّدِيدَ اليَوم
3. الا تَشْعُرُ بِالْوَعْي بِشَأْنِ الوَقْتِ؟

<u>English translation</u>

1. I felt a pain in my stomach.
2. I feel very grateful today.
3. Do you not feel conscious of the time?

Verb #77 - فَتَحَ – to open, to unlock, to conquer

الضَّمِير (Pronoun)	الْمَاضِى (Past)	الْمُضَارع (Present)	أَمْر (Imperative)	الْمَصْدَر (Verbal Noun)	إِسْم الْفَاعِل (The active participle)	إِسْم الْمَفْعُول (The passive participle)
هُوَ	فَتَحَ	يَفْتَحُ		فَتْح	فَاتِح	مَفْتُوح
هُمَا	فَتَحَا	يَفْتَحَانِ				
هُمْ	فَتَحُوا	يَفْتَحُونَ				
هِيَ	فَتَحَتْ	تَفْتَحُ				
هُمَا	فَتَحَتَا	تَفْتَحَانِ				
هُنَّ	فَتَحْنَ	يَفْتَحْنَ				
أَنْتَ	فَتَحْتَ	تَفْتَحُ	اِفْتَحْ			
أَنْتُمَا	فَتَحْتُمَا	تَفْتَحَانِ	اِفْتَحَا			
أَنْتُمْ	فَتَحْتُمْ	تَفْتَحُونَ	اِفْتَحُوا			
أَنْتِ	فَتَحْتِ	تَفْتَحِينَ	اِفْتَحِي			
أَنْتُمَا	فَتَحْتُمَا	تَفْتَحَانِ	اِفْتَحَا			
أَنْتُنَّ	فَتَحْتُنَّ	تَفْتَحْنَ	اِفْتَحْنَ			
أَنَا	فَتَحْتُ	أَفْتَحُ				
نَحْنُ	فَتَحْنَا	نَفْتَحُ				

Sentences

1.فَتَحْتُ البَابَ بِصُعُوبَةٍ

2.هَلْ سَمِعْتُم بِفَتْح مَكَّة؟

3.فَتَحْتُ مِقْبَضَ البَاب

English translation

1. I opened the door with difficulty.
2. Have you heard about the conquest of Mecca?
3. I unlocked/opened the door handle.

Verb #78 – شَهِدَ – to witness, to testify, to attest

اِسْم الْمَفْعُول (The passive participle)	اِسْم الْفَاعِل (The active participle)	الْمَصْدَر (Verbal Noun)	أَمْرُ (Imperative)	الْمُضَارِع (Present)	الْمَاضِي (Past)	الضَّمِير (pronoun)
مَشْهُود	شَاهِد	شُهُود		يَشْهَدُ / يَشْهَدَانِ / يَشْهَدُونَ	شَهِدَ / شَهِدَا / شَهِدُوا	هُوَ / هُمَا / هُمْ
				تَشْهَدُ / تَشْهَدَانِ / يَشْهَدْنَ	شَهِدَتْ / شَهِدَتَا / شَهِدْنَ	هِيَ / هُمَا / هُنَّ
			اِشْهَدْ / اِشْهَدَا / اِشْهَدُوا	تَشْهَدُ / تَشْهَدَانِ / تَشْهَدُونَ	شَهِدْتَ / شَهِدْتُمَا / شَهِدْتُمْ	أَنْتَ / أَنْتُمَا / أَنْتُمْ
			اِشْهَدِي / اِشْهَدَا / اِشْهَدْنَ	تَشْهَدِينَ / تَشْهَدَانِ / تَشْهَدْنَ	شَهِدْتِ / شَهِدْتُمَا / شَهِدْتُنَّ	أَنْتِ / أَنْتُمَا / أَنْتُنَّ
				أَشْهَدُ / نَشْهَدُ	شَهِدْتُ / شَهِدْنَا	أَنَا / نَحْنُ

Sentences

1. أَشْهَدُ عَلى نَجاحِكَ

2. هَلْ كُنْتَ شَاهِدً عِنْدَمَا حَدَثَ ذَلِكَ؟

3. تَطْلُبُ الشُرْطَةَ مِن الشُهُود الذين كَانُو هُنَاكَ

English translation

1. I testify to your success.
2. Where you a witness when that happened?
3. The police are asking for witnesses who were there.

Verb #79 – مَاتَ – to die, to perish, to pass away

اِسْم الْمَفْعُول (The passive participle)	اِسْم الْفَاعِل (The active participle)	الْمَصْدَر (Verbal Noun)	أَمْر (Imperative)	الْمُضَارِع (Present)	الْمَاضِي (Past)	الضَّمِير (pronoun)
مَمُوت	مَائِت	مَوْت		يَمُوتُ يَمُوتَانِ يَمُوتُونَ	مَاتَ مَاتَا مَاتُوا	هُوَ هُمَا هُمْ
				تَمُوتُ تَمُوتَانِ يَمُتْنَ	مَاتَتْ مَاتَتَا مُتْنَ	هِيَ هُمَا هُنَّ
			مُتْ مُوتَا مُوتُوا	تَمُوتُ تَمُوتَانِ تَمُوتُونَ	مُتَّ مُتُّمَا مُتُّمْ	أَنْتَ أَنْتُمَا أَنْتُمْ
			مُوتِى مُوتَا مُتْنَ	تَمُوتِينَ تَمُوتَانِ تَمُتْنَ	مُتِّ مُتُّمَا مُتُّنَّ	أَنْتِ أَنْتُمَا أَنْتُنَّ
				أَمُوتُ نَمُوتُ	مُتُّ مُتْنَا	أَنَا نَحْنُ

Sentences

مَاتَ الطِفْل مِن قَبل أَنْ يُوْلَد.1
سَيَذُوقُ كُّلَ شَخْصٍ المَوتَ.2
كُلَّ خَلْقٍ سَيَمُوتُ في نِهَايَةِ المَطَافِ.3

English translation

1. The child died before he was born.
2. Everybody will taste death.
3. Every creation will eventually perish.

Verb #80 – فَهِمَ – to understand, to comprehend

اِسْم الْمَفْعُول (The passive participle)	اِسْم الْفَاعِل (The active participle)	الْمَصْدَر (Verbal Noun)	أَمْرٌ (Imperative)	الْمُضَارِع (Present)	الْمَاضِي (Past)	الضَّمِير (pronoun)
مَفْهُوم	فَاهِم	فَهْم		يَفْهَمُ / يَفْهَمَانِ / يَفْهَمُونَ	فَهِمَ / فَهِمَا / فَهِمُوا	هُوَ / هُمَا / هُمْ
				تَفْهَمُ / تَفْهَمَانِ / يَفْهَمْنَ	فَهِمَتْ / فَهِمَتَا / فَهِمْنَ	هِيَ / هُمَا / هُنَّ
			اِفْهَمْ / اِفْهَمَا / اِفْهَمُوا	تَفْهَمُ / تَفْهَمَانِ / تَفْهَمُونَ	فَهِمْتَ / فَهِمْتُمَا / فَهِمْتُمْ	أَنْتَ / أَنْتُمَا / أَنْتُمْ
			اِفْهَمِي / اِفْهَمَا / اِفْهَمْنَ	تَفْهَمِينَ / تَفْهَمَانِ / تَفْهَمْنَ	فَهِمْتِ / فَهِمْتُمَا / فَهِمْتُنَّ	أَنْتِ / أَنْتُمَا / أَنْتُنَّ
				أَفْهَمُ / نَفْهَمُ	فَهِمْتُ / فَهِمْنَا	أَنَا / نَحْنُ

Sentences

1.فَهِمْتُ الدَّرْسَ جَيِّداً

2.فَهْمُ العُلُومِ سَهْلٌ

3.بَعْضُ النَّاسِ يَفْهَمُون أَفْضَلُ مِن الأَخَرِينَ

English translation

1. I understood the lesson well.

2. Understanding science is easy.

3. Some people are able to comprehend better than others.

Verb #81 – قَتَلَ – to kill, to murder

اِسْم الْمَفْعُول (The passive participle)	اِسْم الْفَاعِل (The active participle)	الْمَصْدَر (Verbal Noun)	أَمْر (Imperative)	الْمُضَارِع (Present)	الْمَاضِي (Past)	الضَّمِير (pronoun)
مَقْتُول	قَاتِل	قَتْل		يَقْتُلُ يَقْتُلَانِ يَقْتُلُونَ	قَتَلَ قَتَلَا قَتَلُوا	هُوَ هُمَا هُمْ
				تَقْتُلُ تَقْتُلَانِ يَقْتُلْنَ	قَتَلَتْ قَتَلَتَا قَتَلْنَ	هِيَ هُمَا هُنَّ
			اُقْتُلْ اُقْتُلَا اُقْتُلُوا	تَقْتُلُ تَقْتُلَانِ تَقْتُلُونَ	قَتَلْتَ قَتَلْتُمَا قَتَلْتُمْ	أَنْتَ أَنْتُمَا أَنْتُمْ
			اُقْتُلِي اُقْتُلَا اُقْتُلْنَ	تَقْتُلِينَ تَقْتُلَانِ تَقْتُلْنَ	قَتَلْتِ قَتَلْتُمَا قَتَلْتُنَّ	أَنْتِ أَنْتُمَا أَنْتُنَّ
				أَقْتُلُ نَقْتُلُ	قَتَلْتُ قَتَلْنَا	أَنَا نَحْنُ

Sentences

١. لا تَقْتُلْ أَيَّ نَفْسٍ!

٢. هَلْ سَمِعْتَ عَن الفَتَى الذي قُتِلَ؟

٣. كَانَ هُنَاكَ مُظَاهَرَةٌ لِمَقْتَلِ جَورج فَلويد.

English translation

1. Do not kill a single soul!
2. Have you heard about the kid that was murdered?
3. There was a demonstration for the murder of Goerge Floyd.

Verb #82 – دَفَعَ – to push, to pay

اِسْم الْمَفْعُول (The passive participle)	اِسْم الْفَاعِل (The active participle)	الْمَصْدَر (Verbal Noun)	أَمْرٌ (Imperative)	الْمُضَارِع (Present)	الْمَاضِي (Past)	الضَّمِير (Pronoun)
مَدْفُوع	دَافِع	دَفْع		يَدْفَعُ / يَدْفَعَانِ / يَدْفَعُونَ	دَفَعَ / دَفَعَا / دَفَعُوا	هُوَ / هُمَا / هُمْ
				تَدْفَعُ / تَدْفَعَانِ / يَدْفَعْنَ	دَفَعَتْ / دَفَعَتَا / دَفَعْنَ	هِيَ / هُمَا / هُنَّ
			اِدْفَعْ / اِدْفَعَا / اِدْفَعُوا	تَدْفَعُ / تَدْفَعَانِ / تَدْفَعُونَ	دَفَعْتَ / دَفَعْتُمَا / دَفَعْتُمْ	أَنْتَ / أَنْتُمَا / أَنْتُمْ
			اِدْفَعِي / اِدْفَعَا / اِدْفَعْنَ	تَدْفَعِينَ / تَدْفَعَانِ / تَدْفَعْنَ	دَفَعْتِ / دَفَعْتُمَا / دَفَعْتُنَّ	أَنْتِ / أَنْتُمَا / أَنْتُنَّ
				أَدْفَعُ / نَدْفَعُ	دَفَعْتُ / دَفَعْنَا	أَنَا / نَحْنُ

Sentences

١. دَفَعْتُ الفَاتُوْرَةَ فِي المَطْعَمِ

٢. دَفَعَ أَحْمَدُ أَخِيهِ اِلى الأَرضِ

٣. دَفَعْتُ السَّيَارَةَ عَلى الطَرِيقِ

English translation

1. I paid the bill at the restaurant.
2. Ahmed pushed his brother to the ground.
3. I pushed the car onto the road.

Verb #83 – نَزَلَ – to come down, to descend

إِسْم الْمَفْعُول (The passive participle)	إِسْم الْفَاعِل (The active participle)	الْمَصْدَر (Verbal Noun)	أَمْرٌ (Imperative)	الْمُضَارِع (Present)	الْمَاضِي (Past)	الضَّمِير (pronoun)
مَنْزُول	نَازِل	نُزُول		يَنْزِلُ / يَنْزِلَانِ / يَنْزِلُونَ	نَزَلَ / نَزَلَا / نَزَلُوا	هُوَ / هُمَا / هُمْ
				تَنْزِلُ / تَنْزِلَانِ / يَنْزِلْنَ	نَزَلَتْ / نَزَلَتَا / نَزَلْنَ	هِيَ / هُمَا / هُنَّ
			اِنْزِلْ / اِنْزِلَا / اِنْزِلُوا	تَنْزِلُ / تَنْزِلَانِ / تَنْزِلُونَ	نَزَلْتَ / نَزَلْتُمَا / نَزَلْتُمْ	أَنْتَ / أَنْتُمَا / أَنْتُمْ
			اِنْزِلِي / اِنْزِلَا / اِنْزِلْنَ	تَنْزِلِينَ / تَنْزِلَانِ / تَنْزِلْنَ	نَزَلْتِ / نَزَلْتُمَا / نَزَلْتُنَّ	أَنْتِ / أَنْتُمَا / أَنْتُنَّ
				أَنْزِلُ / نَنْزِلُ	نَزَلْتُ / نَزَلْنَا	أَنَا / نَحْنُ

<u>Sentences</u>

١.بَدَأَ المَطَرُ أَنْ يَنْزِلَ

٢.نَزَلَتْ الْمَلائِكَةُ

٣.هَلْ نَزَلَ أَىَّ شَخْصٍ هُنَا؟

<u>English translation</u>

1. The rain started coming down.
2. The angels descended.
3. Has anybody come down here?

Verb #84 – بَحَثَ – to search for, to examine (comes with عَنْ)

اِسْم الْمَفْعُول (The passive participle)	اِسْم الْفَاعِل (The active participle)	الْمَصْدَر (Verbal Noun)	أَمْر (Imperative)	الْمُضَارِع (Present)	الْمَاضِي (Past)	الضّمِير (pronoun)
مَبْحُوث	بَاحِث	بَحْث		يَبْحَثُ يَبْحَثَانِ يَبْحَثُونَ	بَحَثَ بَحَثَا بَحَثُوا	هُوَ هُمَا هُمْ
				تَبْحَثُ تَبْحَثَانِ يَبْحَثْنَ	بَحَثَتْ بَحَثَتَا بَحَثْنَ	هِيَ هُمَا هُنَّ
			اِبْحَثْ اِبْحَثَا اِبْحَثُوا	تَبْحَثُ تَبْحَثَانِ تَبْحَثُونَ	بَحَثْتَ بَحَثْتُمَا بَحَثْتُمْ	أَنْتَ أَنْتُمَا أَنْتُمْ
			اِبْحَثِي اِبْحَثَا اِبْحَثْنَ	تَبْحَثِينَ تَبْحَثَانِ تَبْحَثْنَ	بَحَثْتِ بَحَثْتُمَا بَحَثْتُنَّ	أَنْتِ أَنْتُمَا أَنْتُنَّ
				أَبْحَثُ نَبْحَثُ	بَحَثْتُ بَحَثْنَا	أَنَا نَحْنُ

Sentences

1. بَحَثْتُ عَن المُعْجَمِ في المَكْتَبةِ.
2. بَحَثَتَا الإمْرَاتَانِ عَن المَعْهَدِ.
3. سَأَبْحَثُ عن النَتَائِج.

English translation

1. I searched for the dictionary in the library.
2. The two women searched for the institute.
3. I will look for/examine the results.

Verb #85 – أَخَذ – to take something

اِسْم الْمَفْعُول (The passive participle)	اِسْم الْفَاعِل (The active participle)	الْمَصْدَر (Verbal Noun)	أَمْر (Imperative)	الْمُضَارِع (Present)	الْمَاضِي (Past)	الضَّمِير (pronoun)
مَأْخُوذ	آخِذ	أَخْذ		يَأْخُذُ يَأْخُذَانِ يَأْخُذُونَ	أَخَذَ أَخَذَا أَخَذُوا	هُوَ هُمَا هُمْ
				تَأْخُذُ تَأْخُذَانِ يَأْخُذْنَ	أَخَذَتْ أَخَذَتَا أَخَذْنَ	هِيَ هُمَا هُنَّ
			خُذْ خُذَا خُذُوا	تَأْخُذُ تَأْخُذَانِ تَأْخُذُونَ	أَخَذْتَ أَخَذْتُمَا أَخَذْتُمْ	أَنْتَ أَنْتُمَا أَنْتُمْ
			خُذِي خُذَا خُذْنَ	تَأْخُذِينَ تَأْخُذَانِ تَأْخُذْنَ	أَخَذْتِ أَخَذْتُمَا أَخَذْتُنَّ	أَنْتِ أَنْتُمَا أَنْتُنَّ
				آخُذُ نَأْخُذُ	أَخَذْتُ أَخَذْنَا	أَنَا نَحْنُ

<u>Sentences</u>

1‎.أَخَذْتُ المَالَ مِنْ أَبِي‎

2‎.لا تَأْخُذْ مَا لا تَخَصُّكَ‎

3‎.خُذْ الخَيْرَ وَاتْرُك السُوءَ‎

<u>English translation</u>

1. I took the money from my father.
2. Do not take what doesn't belong to you.
3. Take the good and leave the bad.

Verb #86 – حَقَّقَ – to achieve, to realize (goals)

اِسْم الْمَفْعُول (The passive participle)	اِسْم الْفَاعِل (The active participle)	الْمَصْدَر (Verbal Noun)	أَمْرّ (Imperative)	الْمُضَارِع (Present)	الْمَاضِي (Past)	الضَّمِير (pronoun)
مُحَقَّق	مُحَقِّق	تَحْقِيق		يُحَقِّقُ يُحَقِّقَانِ يُحَقِّقُونَ	حَقَّقَ حَقَّقَا حَقَّقُوا	هُوَ هُمَا هُمْ
				تُحَقِّقُ تُحَقِّقَانِ يُحَقِّقْنَ	حَقَّقَتْ حَقَّقَتَا حَقَّقْنَ	هِيَ هُمَا هُنَّ
			حَقِّقْ حَقِّقَا حَقِّقُوا	تُحَقِّقُ تُحَقِّقَانِ تُحَقِّقُونَ	حَقَّقْتَ حَقَّقْتُمَا حَقَّقْتُمْ	أَنْتَ أَنْتُمَا أَنْتُمْ
			حَقِّقِي حَقِّقَا حَقِّقْنَ	تُحَقِّقِينَ تُحَقِّقَانِ تُحَقِّقْنَ	حَقَّقْتِ حَقَّقْتُمَا حَقَّقْتُنَّ	أَنْتِ أَنْتُمَا أَنْتُنَّ
				أَحَقِّقُ نُحَقِّقُ	حَقَّقْتُ حَقَّقْنَا	أَنَا نَحْنُ

<u>Sentences</u>

1. حَقَّقْتُ نَجَاحَاً كَبِيراً العَام الْمَاضِي
2. التَحْقِيق يَسْتَنِدُ إِلى العَمَل الشَّاقّ
3. تَحَقَّقْ أَهْدَافك مِنْ وَقْتٍ مُبَكِّر

<u>English translation</u>

1. I achieved great success last year.
2. Achieving is based on hard work.
3. Realize your goals from early.

Verb #87 – رَفَضَ – to reject, to refuse

اِسْم الْمَفْعُول (The passive participle)	اِسْم الْفَاعِل (The active participle)	الْمَصْدَر (Verbal Noun)	أَمْرٌ (Imperative)	الْمُضَارِع (Present)	الْمَاضِي (Past)	الضَّمِير (pronoun)
مَرْفُوض	رَافِض	رَفْض		يَرْفُضُ / يَرْفُضَانِ / يَرْفُضُونَ	رَفَضَ / رَفَضَا / رَفَضُوا	هُوَ / هُمَا / هُمْ
				تَرْفُضُ / تَرْفُضَانِ / يَرْفُضْنَ	رَفَضَتْ / رَفَضَتَا / رَفَضْنَ	هِيَ / هُمَا / هُنَّ
			اِرْفُضْ / اِرْفُضَا / اِرْفُضُوا	تَرْفُضُ / تَرْفُضَانِ / تَرْفُضُونَ	رَفَضْتَ / رَفَضْتُمَا / رَفَضْتُمْ	أَنْتَ / أَنْتُمَا / أَنْتُمْ
			اِرْفُضِي / اِرْفُضَا / اِرْفُضْنَ	تَرْفُضِينَ / تَرْفُضَانِ / تَرْفُضْنَ	رَفَضْتِ / رَفَضْتُمَا / رَفَضْتُنَّ	أَنْتِ / أَنْتُمَا / أَنْتُنَّ
				أَرْفُضُ / نَرْفُضُ	رَفَضْتُ / رَفَضْنَا	أَنَا / نَحْنُ

Sentences

1. رَفَضَ الرَجُلُ أَنْ يَدْفَعَ فَاتُورَةَ الهَاتِف
2. رُفِضَتْ بِطَاقَتَهُ فِي جِهَازِ الصَّرَّافِ
3. رَفَضَتْ الْأُمُّ الِاقْتِرَاحَ الْمُتَعَلِّقِ بِابْنَتِهَا

English translation

1. The man refused to pay the phone bill.
2. His card was rejected in the ATM machine.
3. The mother rejected the proposal for her daughter.

Verb #88 – اِتَّصَلَ – to contact (mostly used with phone)

اِسْم الْمَفْعُول (The passive participle)	اِسْم الْفَاعِل (The active participle)	الْمَصْدَر (Verbal Noun)	أَمْر (Imperative)	الْمُضَارِع (Present)	الْمَاضِي (Past)	الضَّمِير (pronoun)
مُتَّصَل	مُتَّصِل	اِتِّصَال		يَتَّصِلُ / يَتَّصِلَانِ / يَتَّصِلُونَ	اِتَّصَلَ / اِتَّصَلَا / اِتَّصَلُوا	هُوَ / هُمَا / هُمْ
				تَتَّصِلُ / تَتَّصِلَانِ / يَتَّصِلْنَ	اِتَّصَلَتْ / اِتَّصَلَتَا / اِتَّصَلْنَ	هِيَ / هُمَا / هُنَّ
			اِتَّصِلْ / اِتَّصِلَا / اِتَّصِلُوا	تَتَّصِلُ / تَتَّصِلَانِ / تَتَّصِلُونَ	اِتَّصَلْتَ / اِتَّصَلْتُمَا / اِتَّصَلْتُمْ	أَنْتَ / أَنْتُمَا / أَنْتُمْ
			اِتَّصِلِي / اِتَّصِلَا / اِتَّصِلْنَ	تَتَّصِلِينَ / تَتَّصِلَانِ / تَتَّصِلْنَ	اِتَّصَلْتِ / اِتَّصَلْتُمَا / اِتَّصَلْتُنَّ	أَنْتِ / أَنْتُمَا / أَنْتُنَّ
				أَتَّصِلُ / نَتَّصِلُ	اِتَّصَلْتُ / اِتَّصَلْنَا	أَنَا / نَحْنُ

Sentences

١. اِتَّصَلْتُ بِوَالِدَتِي لِأَوَّلِ مَرَّة مُنْذُ سَنَةٍ.

٢. اِتَّصَلَتْ إيْمِي بِصَدِيقَتِهَا طَلَبًا لِلْمُسَاعَدَةِ.

٣. لا تَخَافُوا مِن الِاتِّصَالِ بِخَطِّ الْمُسَاعَدَةِ.

English translation

1. I contacted my mother for the first time in a year.
2. Amy called/contacted her friend for help.
3. Do not be afraid to contact the help line.

Verb #89 – قَرَّرَ – to decide, to settle

اِسْم الْمَفْعُول (The passive participle)	اِسْم الْفَاعِل (The active participle)	الْمَصْدَر (Verbal Noun)	أَمْرّ (Imperative)	الْمُضَارِع (Present)	الْمَاضِي (Past)	الضَّمِير (pronoun)
مُقَرَّر	مُقَرِّر	تَقْرِير		يُقَرِّرُ	قَرَّرَ	هُوَ
				يُقَرِّرَانِ	قَرَّرَا	هُمَا
				يُقَرِّرُونَ	قَرَّرُوا	هُمْ
				تُقَرِّرُ	قَرَّرَتْ	هِيَ
				تُقَرِّرَانِ	قَرَّرَتَا	هُمَا
				يُقَرِّرْنَ	قَرَّرْنَ	هُنَّ
			قَرِّرْ	تُقَرِّرُ	قَرَّرْتَ	أَنْتَ
			قَرِّرَا	تُقَرِّرَانِ	قَرَّرْتُمَا	أَنْتُمَا
			قَرِّرُوا	تُقَرِّرُونَ	قَرَّرْتُمْ	أَنْتُمْ
			قَرِّرِي	تُقَرِّرِينَ	قَرَّرْتِ	أَنْتِ
			قَرِّرَا	تُقَرِّرَانِ	قَرَّرْتُمَا	أَنْتُمَا
			قَرِّرْنَ	تُقَرِّرْنَ	قَرَّرْتُنَّ	أَنْتُنَّ
				أُقَرِّرُ	قَرَّرْتُ	أَنَا
				نُقَرِّرُ	قَرَّرْنَا	نَحْنُ

Sentences

1.قَرَّرْتُ أَنَّنِي لَاَ أُرِيدُ الْإِنْضِمَامَ اِلى الصَّفِ

2.الاِسْتِقْرَارُ فِي أُرُوبَا أَمْرٌ صَعَبٌ

3.لا تُقَرِّرْ بِهَذِه السُرْعَةِ، خُذْ وَقْتَكَ

English translation

1. I decided that I do not want to join the class.
2. Settling in Europe is difficult.
3. Do not decide so quickly, take your time.

Verb #90 – كَشَفَ – discover, to uncover

اِسْم الْمَفْعُول (The passive participle)	اِسْم الْفَاعِل (The active participle)	الْمَصْدَر (Verbal Noun)	أَمْر (Imperative)	الْمُضَارِع (Present)	الْمَاضِي (Past)	الضَّمِير (Pronoun)
مَكْشُوف	كَاشِف	كَشْف		يَكْشِفُ / يَكْشِفَانِ / يَكْشِفُونَ	كَشَفَ / كَشَفَا / كَشَفُوا	هُوَ / هُمَا / هُمْ
				تَكْشِفُ / تَكْشِفَانِ / يَكْشِفْنَ	كَشَفَتْ / كَشَفَتَا / كَشَفْنَ	هِيَ / هُمَا / هُنَّ
			اِكْشِفْ / اِكْشِفَا / اِكْشِفُوا	تَكْشِفُ / تَكْشِفَانِ / تَكْشِفُونَ	كَشَفْتَ / كَشَفْتُمَا / كَشَفْتُمْ	أَنْتَ / أَنْتُمَا / أَنْتُمْ
			اِكْشِفِي / اِكْشِفَا / اِكْشِفْنَ	تَكْشِفِينَ / تَكْشِفَانِ / تَكْشِفْنَ	كَشَفْتِ / كَشَفْتُمَا / كَشَفْتُنَّ	أَنْتِ / أَنْتُمَا / أَنْتُنَّ
				أَكْشِفُ / نَكْشِفُ	كَشَفْتُ / كَشَفْنَا	أَنَا / نَحْنُ

Sentences

1.كَشَفْتُ تِلْكَ المَعْلُومَات مُنْذُ فَتْرَةٍ

2.سَتَجِدُ بَعْضَ الِاكْتِشَافَاتِ الغَرِيبَة هُنَاكَ

3.كَشَفْتُ الحِسَابَات حَيْثُ عُمَّالُ الْمُتَاجِرِين كَانُوا يُوَصِلُونَ المَالَ

English translation

1. I discovererd that information a while ago.
2. You will find the weirdest discoveries over there.
3. I uncovered the accounts where the shopkeepers were laundering the money.

Verb #91 – سَمَحَ – to allow, to permit

اِسْم الْمَفْعُول (The passive participle)	اِسْم الْفَاعِل (The active participle)	الْمَصْدَر (Verbal Noun)	أَمْرٌ (Imperative)	الْمُضَارِع (Present)	الْمَاضِي (Past)	الضَّمِير (pronoun)
مَسْمُوح	سَامِح	سَمَاح		يَسْمَحُ / يَسْمَحَانِ / يَسْمَحُونَ	سَمَحَ / سَمَحَا / سَمَحُوا	هُوَ / هُمَا / هُمْ
				تَسْمَحُ / تَسْمَحَانِ / يَسْمَحْنَ	سَمَحَتْ / سَمَحَتَا / سَمَحْنَ	هِيَ / هُمَا / هُنَّ
			اِسْمَحْ / اِسْمَحَا / اِسْمَحُوا	تَسْمَحُ / تَسْمَحَانِ / تَسْمَحُونَ	سَمَحْتَ / سَمَحْتُمَا / سَمَحْتُمْ	أَنْتَ / أَنْتُمَا / أَنْتُمْ
			اِسْمَحِي / اِسْمَحَا / اِسْمَحْنَ	تَسْمَحِينَ / تَسْمَحَانِ / تَسْمَحْنَ	سَمَحْتِ / سَمَحْتُمَا / سَمَحْتُنَّ	أَنْتِ / أَنْتُمَا / أَنْتُنَّ
				أَسْمَحُ / نَسْمَحُ	سَمَحْتُ / سَمَحْنَا	أَنَا / نَحْنُ

Sentences

1. الْخُطُوطُ الْجَوِيَّةُ سَمَحُوا لِي بِالسَفَرِ

2. اِسْمَحْ لِي أَنْ أَعْرِضَ نَفْسِي

3. لا تَسْمَحْ بِحُدُوثِ ذَلِكَ مَرَّةً أُخْرَى

English translation

1. The airlines permitted me to travel.
2. Allow me to introduce myself
3. Don't allow that to happen again.

Verb #92 – سَامَحَ – to forgive, to pardon

اِسْم الْمَفْعُول (The passive participle)	اِسْم الْفَاعِل (The active participle)	الْمَصْدَر (Verbal Noun)	أَمْر (Imperative)	الْمُضَارِع (Present)	الْمَاضِي (Past)	الضَّمِير (pronoun)
مُسَامَح	مُسَامِح	مُسَامَحَة		يُسَامِحُ / يُسَامِحَانِ / يُسَامِحُونَ	سَامَحَ / سَامَحَا / سَامَحُوا	هُوَ / هُمَا / هُمْ
				تُسَامِحُ / تُسَامِحَانِ / يُسَامِحْنَ	سَامَحَتْ / سَامَحَتَا / سَامَحْنَ	هِيَ / هُمَا / هُنَّ
			سَامِحْ / سَامِحَا / سَامِحُوا	تُسَامِحُ / تُسَامِحَانِ / تُسَامِحُونَ	سَامَحْتَ / سَامَحْتُمَا / سَامَحْتُمْ	أَنْتَ / أَنْتُمَا / أَنْتُمْ
			سَامِحِي / سَامِحَا / سَامِحْنَ	تُسَامِحِينَ / تُسَامِحَانِ / تُسَامِحْنَ	سَامَحْتِ / سَامَحْتُمَا / سَامَحْتُنَّ	أَنْتِ / أَنْتُمَا / أَنْتُنَّ
				أُسَامِحُ / نُسَامِحُ	سَامَحْتُ / سَامَحْنَا	أَنَا / نَحْنُ

Sentences

1.سَامِحْنِي عَلى أُسْلُوبِي السَّيِّئَةِ

2.إِنَّ عَمَلَ المُسَامَحَة مُهِّمٌ لِلغَايَةِ

3.كَيْفَ يُمْكِنُنِي أَنْ أُسَامِحَهُ عَلى ذَلِكَ؟

English translation

1. Forgive me for my bad manners.
2. The act of forgiveness is extremely important.
3. How can I forgive him for that?

Verb #93 – حَضَرَ – to be present, to attend

اِسْم الْمَفْعُول (The passive participle)	اِسْم الْفَاعِل (The active participle)	الْمَصْدَر (Verbal Noun)	أَمْر (Imperative)	الْمُضَارِع (Present)	الْمَاضِي (Past)	الضَّمِير (pronoun)
مَحْضُور	حَاضِر	حُضُور		يَحْضُر	حَضَرَ	هُوَ
				يَحْضُرَان	حَضَرَا	هُمَا
				يَحْضُرُونَ	حَضَرُوا	هُم
				تَحْضُر	حَضَرَتْ	هِيَ
				تَحْضُرَان	حَضَرَتَا	هُمَا
				يَحْضُرْنَ	حَضَرْنَ	هُنَّ
			أَحْضُر	تَحْضُر	حَضَرْتَ	أَنْتَ
			أَحْضُرَا	تَحْضُرَان	حَضَرْتُمَا	أَنْتُمَا
			أَحْضُرُوا	تَحْضُرُونَ	حَضَرْتُمْ	أَنْتُمْ
			أَحْضُرِي	تَحْضُرِينَ	حَضَرْتِ	أَنْتِ
			أَحْضُرَا	تَحْضُرَان	حَضَرْتُمَا	أَنْتُمَا
			أَحْضُرْنَ	تَحْضُرْنَ	حَضَرْتُنَّ	أَنْتُنَّ
				أَحْضُر	حَضَرْتُ	أَنَا
				نَحْضُر	حَضَرْنَا	نَحْنُ

Sentences

1. أُحْضُرِ الدَّرْسَ في الوَقْتِ لْمُحَدَّدِ.
2. كُنْتُ حَاضِراً في الِاجْتِمَاع.
3. لَا أُحِبُّ حُضُورَ المَتْحَفِ.

English translation

1. Attend the lesson in the designated time.
2. I was present at the meeting.
3. I don't like attending the museum.

Verb #94 – مَلَكَ – to possess something, to own something

اِسْم الْمَفْعُول (The passive participle)	اِسم الْفَاعِل (The active participle)	الْمَصْدَر (Verbal Noun)	أَمْرٌ (Imperative)	الْمُضَارِع (Present)	الْمَاضِي (Past)	الضَّمِير (pronoun)
مَمْلُوك	مَالِك	مَلْك		يَمْلِكُ يَمْلِكَانِ يَمْلِكُونَ	مَلَكَ مَلَكَا مَلَكُوا	هُوَ هُمَا هُمْ
				تَمْلِكُ تَمْلِكَانِ يَمْلِكْنَ	مَلَكَتْ مَلَكَتَا مَلَكْنَ	هِيَ هُمَا هُنَّ
			اِمْلِكْ اِمْلِكَا اِمْلِكُوا	تَمْلِكُ تَمْلِكَانِ تَمْلِكُونَ	مَلَكْتَ مَلَكْتُمَا مَلَكْتُمْ	أَنْتَ أَنْتُمَا أَنْتُمْ
			اِمْلِكِي اِمْلِكَا اِمْلِكْنَ	تَمْلِكِينَ تَمْلِكَانِ تَمْلِكْنَ	مَلَكْتِ مَلَكْتُمَا مَلَكْتُنَّ	أَنْتِ أَنْتُمَا أَنْتُنَّ
				أَمْلِكُ نَمْلِكُ	مَلَكْتُ مَلَكْنَا	أَنَا نَحْنُ

<u>Sentences</u>

١.أَنَا لا أَمْلِكُ كَثِيراً مِن المَالِ

٢.كَانَ الرَجُلَانِ يَمْلِكَانِ العَقَّار

٣.لَا شَيْءَ يَخُصّكَ، حَتَّى تَمْلِكَهُ

<u>English translation</u>

1. I don't possess a lot of money.
2. The two men owned the property.
3. Nothing belongs to you, until you own it.

Verb #95 – نَقَلَ – to move something, to transport something

إِسْم الْمَفْعُول (The passive participle)	إِسْم الْفَاعِل (The active participle)	الْمَصْدَر (Verbal Noun)	أَمْرٌ (Imperative)	الْمُضَارِع (Present)	الْمَاضِي (Past)	الضَّمِير (pronoun)
مَنْقُول	نَاقِل	نَقْل		يَنْقُلُ يَنْقُلَانِ يَنْقُلُونَ	نَقَلَ نَقَلَا نَقَلُوا	هُوَ هُمَا هُمْ
				تَنْقُلُ تَنْقُلَانِ يَنْقُلْنَ	نَقَلَتْ نَقَلَتَا نَقَلْنَ	هِيَ هُمَا هُنَّ
			أُنْقُلْ أُنْقُلَا أُنْقُلُوا	تَنْقُلُ تَنْقُلَانِ تَنْقُلُونَ	نَقَلْتَ نَقَلْتُمَا نَقَلْتُمْ	أَنْتَ أَنْتُمَا أَنْتُمْ
			أُنْقُلِي أُنْقُلَا أُنْقُلْنَ	تَنْقُلِينَ تَنْقُلَانِ تَنْقُلْنَ	نَقَلْتِ نَقَلْتُمَا نَقَلْتُنَّ	أَنْتِ أَنْتُمَا أَنْتُنَّ
				أَنْقُلُ نَنْقُلُ	نَقَلْتُ نَقَلْنَا	أَنَا نَحْنُ

Sentences

1.نَقَلْتُ الصَّنَادِيقِ اِلى غُرْفَتِي.

2.تَمَّ نَقْلَ الكُتُب مِنْ البَرَازِيل.

3.لا يُمْكِنُنِي أَنْ أَكُونَ مَنْقُولٌ اَلى الْيَابَانِ.

English translation

1. I moved the boxes into my room.
2. The books were transported from Brazil.
3. I cannot be transferred to japan.

Verb #96 – عَقَدَ – to tie, to hold, to covenant/contract

اِسْم الْمَفْعُول (The passive participle)	اِسْم الْفَاعِل (The active participle)	الْمَصْدَر (Verbal Noun)	أَمْر (Imperative)	الْمُضَارِع (Present)	الْمَاضِي (Past)	الضَّمِير (pronoun)
مَعْقُود	عَاقِد	عَقْد		يَعْقِدُ / يَعْقِدَانِ / يَعْقِدُونَ	عَقَدَ / عَقَدَا / عَقَدُوا	هُوَ / هُمَا / هُمْ
				تَعْقِدُ / تَعْقِدَانِ / يَعْقِدْنَ	عَقَدَتْ / عَقَدَتَا / عَقَدْنَ	هِيَ / هُمَا / هُنَّ
			اِعْقِدْ / اِعْقِدَا / اِعْقِدُوا	تَعْقِدُ / تَعْقِدَانِ / تَعْقِدُونَ	عَقَدْتَ / عَقَدْتُمَا / عَقَدْتُمْ	أَنْتَ / أَنْتُمَا / أَنْتُمْ
			اِعْقِدِي / اِعْقِدَا / اِعْقِدْنَ	تَعْقِدِينَ / تَعْقِدَانِ / تَعْقِدْنَ	عَقَدْتِ / عَقَدْتُمَا / عَقَدْتُنَّ	أَنْتِ / أَنْتُمَا / أَنْتُنَّ
				أَعْقِدُ / نَعْقِدُ	عَقَدْتُ / عَقَدْنَا	أَنَا / نَحْنُ

Sentences

1. عَقَدْتُ الهَاتِفَ في يَدِي
2. لَقَدْ عَقَدْتُ العُقْدَةَ
3. كَانَ هُنَاكَ عَقْدٌ بَينَنَا

Eanglish translation

1. I held the phone in my hands.
2. I tied the knot.
3. There was a covenant/contract between us.

Verb #97 – سَارَ – to march, to step along, to walk

اِسْم الْمَفْعُول (The passive participle)	اِسْم الْفَاعِل (The active participle)	الْمَصْدَر (Verbal Noun)	أَمْرٌ (Imperative)	الْمُضَارِع (Present)	الْمَاضِي (Past)	الضَّمِير (pronoun)
مَسِير	سَائِر	سَيْر		يَسِيرُ / يَسِيرَانِ / يَسِيرُونَ	سَارَ / سَارَا / سَارُوا	هُوَ / هُمَا / هُمْ
				تَسِيرُ / تَسِيرَانِ / يَسِرْنَ	سَارَتْ / سَارَتَا / سِرْنَ	هِيَ / هُمَا / هُنَّ
			سِرْ / سِيرَا / سِيرُوا	تَسِيرُ / تَسِيرَانِ / تَسِيرُونَ	سِرْتَ / سِرْتُمَا / سِرْتُمْ	أَنْتَ / أَنْتُمَا / أَنْتُمْ
			سِيرِي / سِيرَا / سِرْنَ	تَسِيرِينَ / تَسِيرَانِ / تَسِرْنَ	سِرْتِ / سِرْتُمَا / سِرْتُنَّ	أَنْتِ / أَنْتُمَا / أَنْتُنَّ
				أَسِيرُ / نَسِيرُ	سِرْتُ / سِرْنَا	أَنَا / نَحْنُ

<u>Sentences</u>

١.سِرْتُ عَبْرَ الشَّارِع

٢.كَانَ الطُّلَّاب يَسِيرُونَ بِغَضَب

٣.هَلْ يُمْكِنُكَ أَنْ تَسِيرَ بِسُرْعَةٍ؟

<u>English translation</u>

1. I walked/marched across the road.
2. The students were marching in anger.
3. Can you walk fast please?

Verb #98 – شَكَرَ – to be thankfull, to be grateful

اِسْم الْمَفْعُول (The passive participle)	اِسْم الْفَاعِل (The active participle)	الْمَصْدَر (Verbal Noun)	أَمْرٌ (Imperative)	الْمُضَارِع (Present)	الْمَاضِي (Past)	الضَّمِير (pronoun)
مَشْكُور	شَاكِر	شُكْر		يَشْكُرُ يَشْكُرَانِ يَشْكُرُونَ	شَكَرَ شَكَرَا شَكَرُوا	هُوَ هُمَا هُمْ
				تَشْكُرُ تَشْكُرَانِ يَشْكُرْنَ	شَكَرَتْ شَكَرَتَا شَكَرْنَ	هِيَ هُمَا هُنَّ
			اُشْكُرْ اُشْكُرَا اُشْكُرُوا	تَشْكُرُ تَشْكُرَانِ تَشْكُرُونَ	شَكَرْتَ شَكَرْتُمَا شَكَرْتُمْ	أَنْتَ أَنْتُمَا أَنْتُمْ
			اُشْكُرِي اُشْكُرَا اُشْكُرْنَ	تَشْكُرِينَ تَشْكُرَانِ تَشْكُرْنَ	شَكَرْتِ شَكَرْتُمَا شَكَرْتُنَّ	أَنْتِ أَنْتُمَا أَنْتُنَّ
				أَشْكُرُ نَشْكُرُ	شَكَرْتُ شَكَرْنَا	أَنَا نَحْنُ

<u>Sentences</u>

١. أُشْكُرْ رَبَّكَ دَائِماً

٢. نَشْكُرُكُم عَلى هَذَا التَّرْحِيب

٣. لَئِن شَكَرْتُمْ لَأَزِيدَنَّكُمْ (Quran, surah Ibrahim, verse 7)

English translation

1. Always be thankful to your lord.
2. We thank you for this welcoming.
3. If you be thankful to me, then I will increase you.

Verb #99 – جَلَسَ – to sit down

اِسْم الْمَفْعُول (The passive participle)	اِسْم الْفَاعِل (The active participle)	الْمَصْدَر (Verbal Noun)	أَمْرٌ (Imperative)	الْمُضَارِع (Present)	الْمَاضِي (Past)	الضَّمِير (pronoun)
مَجْلُوس	جَالِس	جُلُوس		يَجْلِسُ / يَجْلِسَانِ / يَجْلِسُونَ	جَلَسَ / جَلَسَا / جَلَسُوا	هُوَ / هُمَا / هُمْ
				تَجْلِسُ / تَجْلِسَانِ / يَجْلِسْنَ	جَلَسَتْ / جَلَسَتَا / جَلَسْنَ	هِيَ / هُمَا / هُنَّ
			اِجْلِسْ / اِجْلِسَا / اِجْلِسُوا	تَجْلِسُ / تَجْلِسَانِ / تَجْلِسُونَ	جَلَسْتَ / جَلَسْتُمَا / جَلَسْتُمْ	أَنْتَ / أَنْتُمَا / أَنْتُمْ
			اِجْلِسِي / اِجْلِسَا / اِجْلِسْنَ	تَجْلِسِينَ / تَجْلِسَانِ / تَجْلِسْنَ	جَلَسْتِ / جَلَسْتُمَا / جَلَسْتُنَّ	أَنْتِ / أَنْتُمَا / أَنْتُنَّ
				أَجْلِسُ / نَجْلِسُ	جَلَسْتُ / جَلَسْنَا	أَنَا / نَحْنُ

<u>Sentences</u>

١. لِمَاذَا جَلَسْتُنَّ هُنَاكَ

٢. هَلْ يُمْكِنُكَ أَنْ تَجْلِسَ فِي الْمَقَاعِدِ الْمُخَصَّصَةِ؟

٣. جَلَسْتُ بَعْدَ يَوْمٍ طَوِيلٍ

<u>English translation</u>

1. Why did you sit over there?
2. Can you please sit on the allocated seats?
3. I sat down after a long day.

Verb #100 – نَجَحَ – to pass, to succeed in something

اِسْم الْمَفْعُول (The passive participle)	اِسْم الْفَاعِل (The active participle)	الْمَصْدَر (Verbal Noun)	أَمْرّ (Imperative)	الْمُضَارِع (Present)	الْمَاضِي (Past)	الضَّمِير (pronoun)
مَنْجُوح	نَاجِح	نَجْح		يَنْجَحُ / يَنْجَحَانِ / يَنْجَحُونَ	نَجَحَ / نَجَحَا / نَجَحُوا	هُوَ / هُمَا / هُمْ
				تَنْجَحُ / تَنْجَحَانِ / يَنْجَحْنَ	نَجَحَتْ / نَجَحَتَا / نَجَحْنَ	هِيَ / هُمَا / هُنَّ
			اِنْجَحْ / اِنْجَحَا / اِنْجَحُوا	تَنْجَحُ / تَنْجَحَانِ / تَنْجَحُونَ	نَجَحْتَ / نَجَحْتُمَا / نَجَحْتُمْ	أَنْتَ / أَنْتُمَا / أَنْتُمْ
			اِنْجَحِي / اِنْجَحَا / اِنْجَحْنَ	تَنْجَحِينَ / تَنْجَحَانِ / تَنْجَحْنَ	نَجَحْتِ / نَجَحْتُمَا / نَجَحْتُنَّ	أَنْتِ / أَنْتُمَا / أَنْتُنَّ
				أَنْجَحُ / نَنْجَحُ	نَجَحْتُ / نَجَحْنَا	أَنَا / نَحْنُ

Sentences

١. أَخْبَرَ الرَجُلُ النَاجِحُ نَتَائِجَهُ لِأُمِّه

٢. ما الذِي جَعَلَكَ تُصْبِحُ نَاجِحاً جِدًّا؟

٣. نَجَحَ الرَجُلُ فِي خِطَّتِهِ

English translation

1. The successful man told his mother his results.
2. What made you become so successful?
3. The man succeeded in his plan.

Verb #101 (Extra) – كَادَ – be about to, almost, nearly

الضَّمِير (pronoun)	الْمَاضِي (Past)	الْمُضَارِع (Present)	أَمْر (Imperative)	الْمَصْدَر (Verbal Noun)	اِسْم الْفَاعِل (The active participle)	اِسْم الْمَفْعُول (The passive participle)
هُوَ هُمَا هُمْ	كَادَ كَادَا كَادُوا	يَكَادُ يَكَادَانِ يَكَادُونَ		كَوْد	كَائِد	مَكُود
هِيَ هُمَا هُنَّ	كَادَتْ كَادَتَا كِدْنَ	تَكَادُ تَكَادَانِ يَكَدْنَ				
أَنْتَ أَنْتُمَا أَنْتُمْ	كِدْتَ كِدْتُمَا كِدْتُمْ	تَكَادُ تَكَادَانِ تَكَادُونَ	كَدْ كَادَا كَادُوا			
أَنْتِ أَنْتُمَا أَنْتُنَّ	كِدْتِ كِدْتُمَا كِدْتُنَّ	تَكَادِينَ تَكَادَانِ تَكَدْنَ	كَادِي كَادَا كَدْنَ			
أَنَا نَحْنُ	كِدْتُ كِدْنَا	أَكَادُ نَكَادُ				

<u>Sentences</u>

1.كِدْتُ أَنْ أَسْقُطَ عَلَى الارضِ
2.تَكَادُ السَّمَاوَاتُ يَتَفَطَّرْنَ مِنْهُ وَتَنشَقُّ الْأَرْضُ وَتَخِرُّ الْجِبَالُ هَدًّا (Quran, surah Maryam, verse 90)
3.كَادَتْ السَّيَّارَة أَنْ تَصْدِمَ الْأَوْلَادَ

<u>English translation</u>

1. I almost fell to the ground.
2. The heavens are about to burst, the earth to split apart, and the mountain to crumble to pieces.
3. The car almost hit the boys.

My final request…

Being a smaller author, reviews help me tremendously!

It would mean the world to me if you could leave a review.

Customer reviews

★★★★★ 5 out of 5

12 customer ratings

5 star		100%
4 star		0%
3 star		0%
2 star		0%
1 star		0%

˅ How does Amazon calculate star ratings?

Review this product

Share your thoughts with other customers

Write a customer review

If you liked reading this book and learned a thing or two, please let me know!

It only takes 30 seconds but means so much to me!

Thank you and I can't wait to see your thought

Conclusion

Thank you for reading and listening to this book. I hope you have benefited from this book and the verb conjugation/sentences. I tried to make them as simple as possible and tried to show you all of the contexts in which the verbs can come in. If you further want to conjugate verbs by yourself, you can do It here - https://conjugator.reverso.net/conjugation-arabic.html

Also, remember that Arabic is a language that requires constant practise, don't give up if you do not get it after one day or two, be consistent in your studies, and I am sure that you will become fluent in no time!

References

Habash, N., 2010. *Introduction to Arabic Natural Language Processing.* 1st ed. Toronto: morgan & claypool, p.3.

Lewis, B. and Lewis, V., 2021. *The Pareto (80-20) principle in language learning - Fluent in 3 months - Language Hacking and Travel Tips.* [online] Fluent in 3 months - Language Hacking and Travel Tips. Available at: https://www.fluentin3months.com/80-20-rule/

British Council, 2017. *Languages for the Future.* [online] The British council, p.10. Available at: <https://www.britishcouncil.org/sites/default/files/languages-for-the-future-report.pdf> [Accessed 25 May 2021].

Audsley, S., 2019. *Top 10 Reasons to Study Arabic.* [online] Phdstudies.com. Available at: <https://www.phdstudies.com/article/top-10-reasons-to-study-arabic/> [Accessed 25 May 2021].

Conjugator.reverso.net. n.d. *Arabic verb conjugation: past, present, participle | Reverso Conjugator.* [online] Available at: <https://conjugator.reverso.net/conjugation-arabic.html> [Accessed 25 May 2021].

www.ingramcontent.com/pod-product-compliance
Lightning Source LLC
LaVergne TN
LVHW081303210726
843509LV00019B/205